Securing India in the Cyber Era

This book explores the geopolitics of the global cyber space to analyse India's cyber security landscape. As conflicts go more online, nation-states are manipulating cyber space to exploit each other's dependence on information, communication and digital technologies. All the major powers have dedicated cyber units to breach computer networks, harvest sensitive data and proprietary information, and disrupt critical national infrastructure operations.

This volume reviews threats to Indian computer networks, analyses the country's policy responses to these threats, and suggests comprehensive measures to build resilience in the system. India constitutes the second largest internet user base in the world, and this expansion of the user base also saw an accompanying rise in cyber crimes. The book discusses how the country can protect this user base, the data-dependent critical infrastructure, build resilient digital payment systems, and answer the challenges of the dark net. It also explores India's cyber diplomacy, as an emerging economy with a large IT industry and a well-established technological base.

Topical and lucid, this book, part of *The Gateway House Guide to India in the 2020s* series, will be of interest to scholars and researchers of cyber security, digital diplomacy, foreign policy, international relations, geopolitics, strategic affairs, defence studies, South Asian politics and international politics.

Sameer Patil is Fellow for International Security Studies at Gateway House: Indian Council on Global Relations. His research encompasses India's national security priorities, cyber security, counterterrorism, and defence industrialisation. At Gateway House, Sameer has participated in the India-Canada Track 1.5 Dialogues and India-U.K. Track 1.5 Cyber Dialogue. Sameer has previously worked at the National Security Council Secretariat in the Prime Minister's Office in New Delhi where he handled counter-terrorism, regional security and Kashmir desks. He was part of the inaugural rounds of the India-U.S. and India-U.K. Strategic Intelligence Dialogues after the 2008 Mumbai attacks. He is also a dissertation advisor at the Indian Naval War College, Goa.

Sameer holds a PhD in international relations from Jawaharlal Nehru University, New Delhi. In 2019, he was a recipient of the Canberra Fellowship, awarded by the Department of Foreign Affairs and Trade, Australia. He was also the recipient of the Junior Research Fellowship from the University Grants Commission for pursuing research in international relations. His views on Indian security issues have featured regularly in *The New York Times, The Washington Post, The Guardian, Financial Times, The Wall Street Journal, Al Jazeera, CNBC, Reuters* and other prominent news agencies.

The Gateway House Guide to India in the 2020s
Series Editor: Manjeet Kripalani, *co-founder*
Gateway House: *Indian Council on Global Relations*

The Gateway House Guide to India in the 2020s explores the connections between India's globalist past to the strengths it has developed as it steps into the future, starting with the decade of the 2020s. The volumes in this series discuss a wide range of topics, which include solutions for energy independence and environmental preservation, exposition of the new frontiers in space and technology, India's trade networks, security, foreign policies, and international relations. Furthermore, the series examines the embedded trading and entrepreneurial communities which are coming together to influence global agenda-setting and institution-building through platforms like the G20 and UN Security Council, where India will take leadership roles in this decade, in the post-COVID-19 pandemic world.

This series appeals to an international audience, and is directed to policy-makers, think tanks, bureaucrats, professionals working in the area of politics; scholars and researchers of political science, international relations, foreign policy, world economy, politics and technology, Asian politics, South Asia studies, and contemporary history; students and the general reader, seeking an understanding of what will drive India's positioning in world affairs.

Securing India in the Cyber Era
Sameer Patil

For more information about this series, please visit: www.routledge.com/The-Gateway-House-Guide-to-India-in-the-2020s/book-series/GHGI20

Securing India in the Cyber Era

Sameer Patil

Routledge
Taylor & Francis Group

LONDON AND NEW YORK

First published 2022
by Routledge
2 Park Square, Milton Park, Abingdon, Oxon OX14 4RN

and by Routledge
605 Third Avenue, New York, NY 10158

Routledge is an imprint of the Taylor & Francis Group, an informa business

© 2022 Gateway House: Indian Council on Global Relations

The right of Sameer Patil to be identified as author of this work has been asserted by him in accordance with sections 77 and 78 of the Copyright, Designs and Patents Act 1988.

All rights reserved. No part of this book may be reprinted or reproduced or utilised in any form or by any electronic, mechanical, or other means, now known or hereafter invented, including photocopying and recording, or in any information storage or retrieval system, without permission in writing from the publishers.

Trademark notice: Product or corporate names may be trademarks or registered trademarks, and are used only for identification and explanation without intent to infringe.

British Library Cataloguing-in-Publication Data
A catalogue record for this book is available from the British Library

Library of Congress Cataloging-in-Publication Data
A catalog record for this book has been requested

ISBN: 978-0-367-54850-6 (hbk)
ISBN: 978-0-367-71612-7 (pbk)
ISBN: 978-1-003-15291-0 (ebk)

DOI: 10.4324/9781003152910

Typeset in Times New Roman
by Apex CoVantage, LLC

For Parisa and Saatvik

Contents

List of figures and tables viii
Acknowledgements ix
Abbreviations x

1 The geopolitics of cyber space 1

2 India's cyber security landscape: vulnerabilities and responses 13

3 Protecting India's critical infrastructure 22

4 Building resilient digital payment systems 33

5 Murky alleys of the deep web 47

6 India's lead in cyber diplomacy 59

Bibliography 67
Index 70

Figures and tables

Figures

2.1	Cyber security incidents in India (2006–2019)	14
2.2	India's cyber security architecture	17

Tables

1.1	Major cyber security incidents worldwide since 2007 (excluding India)	3
2.1	Major cyber security incidents involving Indian computer networks	15
3.1	Critical sectors and types of threats	23
4.1	India's digital payment nodes	34
4.2	Vulnerabilities, channels and perpetrators	38
4.3	Regulations governing digital payments	43
5.1	Tools and technologies of the deep web	49
5.2	Evolution of major dark net marketplaces and major crackdowns against them	51
6.1	India's cyber interactions	62

Acknowledgements

There are very few occasions when we are able to thank and acknowledge the help of people like our friends, co-workers, seniors or mentors, and everyone else who strives to help us grow through their efforts, in one way or another. I am grateful to all those who contributed to making sure I was able to complete this book.

First and foremost, without the support of Manjeet Kripalani and Ambassador Neelam Deo, the co-founders of Gateway House, this book would not have seen the light of the day. Their constant encouragement and guidance have been the single most important factor in finishing this book.

Gateway House provided not only a rich and stimulating environment, but a broader view of my field. For that, I am thankful to my colleagues – Amit, Chaitanya, Sifra and Cdr Godbole. I want to particularly mention Ali, Ambika and Sagnik for lending me their time and ears whenever required. A word of encouragement also came from Ambassador Rajiv Bhatia, Blaise Fernandes and Satish Kamat.

I am also thankful to Akshay, Rajni, Karan, Dev, Kunal and Nikhil who provided feedback throughout the research. I am indebted to Dr Samir Saran and K. N. Vaidyanathan, who gave me the opportunity from time to time to present my research in various forums and benefit from the discussions therein. Furthermore, I am thankful to Aijaz, Naresh and Arun, who stepped in whenever there was any personal or professional trouble.

I also want to acknowledge the research assistance provided by Kunal Thakkar for this book. Thanks also to Celine, who makes sure every time that I comply with all the procedures and formalities.

I am grateful to my parents, who encouraged me to take up this field and supported all my endeavours. My brother Prasad spotted my early interest in technology and nurtured it.

Lastly, I owe much gratitude to my wife, Sanghavi, who has shown a tremendous amount of patience and support in my pursuit of professional endeavours. She has stood with me resolutely through thick and thin. Needless to say, I alone take responsibility for any mistakes in the pages that follow.

I dedicate this book to my kids Parisa and Saatvik. I hope that they will be able to see a much safer and more resilient cyber space in the future than what I have written about in this book.

Abbreviations

AEPS	Aadhaar-Enabled Payment Systems
AI	Artificial Intelligence
APT	Advanced Persistent Threat
ATM	Automated Teller Machine
BRICS	Brazil, Russia, India, China and South Africa
C-DAC	Centre for Development of Advanced Computing
CERT-IN	Indian Computer Emergency Response Team
CIRP	Committee on Internet-Related Policies
CMS	Central Monitoring System
DDoS	Distributed Denial of Service
ERNET	Education and Research Network
FBI	Federal Bureau of Investigation
GFCE	Global Forum on Cyber Expertise
GGE	Group of Governmental Experts
I4C	Indian Cyber Crime Coordination Centre
IB-CART	Indian Banks – Center for Analysis of Risks and Threats
ICANN	Internet Corporation for Assigned Names and Numbers
IDRBT	Institute for Development & Research in Banking Technology
IP	Internet Protocol
ISP	Internet Service Provider
IT	Information Technology
ITEC	Indian Technical and Economic Cooperation
ITU	International Telecommunications Union
MEA	Ministry of External Affairs
MEITY	Ministry of Electronics and Information Technology
MHA	Ministry of Home Affairs
MoD	Ministry of Defence
MoF	Ministry of Finance
NCB	Narcotics Control Bureau
NCIIPC	National Critical Information Infrastructure Protection Centre
NCSC	National Cyber Security Coordinator
NCSP	National Cyber Security Policy
NFS	National Financial Switch

NPCI	National Payments Corporation of India
NSA	National Security Agency
NSCS	National Security Council Secretariat
NTRO	National Technical Research Organisation
PGP	Pretty Good Privacy
PoS	Point of Sale
PPI	Prepaid Payment Instrument
RBI	Reserve Bank of India
ReBIT	Reserve Bank Information Technology Private Limited
SCADA	Supervisory Control and Data Acquisition
SOC	Security Operations Centre
SWIFT	Society for Worldwide Interbank Financial Telecommunication
TOR	The Onion Router
UIDAI	Unique Identification Authority of India
UN	United Nations
UPI	Unified Payments Interface
USSD	Unstructured Supplementary Service Data
VPN	Virtual Private Network
WSIS	World Summit on the Information Society
WTO	World Trade Organization

1 The geopolitics of cyber space

Introduction

Cyber space has become the newest and most prominent arena for geopolitical contestations. Nation-states are exploiting each other's dependence on information, communication and digital technologies to breach computer networks, harvest sensitive data and proprietary information, and disrupt critical national infrastructure operations. Today, all the major powers have dedicated cyber units which map out their adversaries' vulnerabilities and capitalise on them.

Consequently, cyber attacks targeting national and commercial computer networks have surged in the last few years. However, 2020 has witnessed a significant expansion of the threat vector and attack techniques, with the outbreak of the COVID-19 pandemic.[1] While global attention is focused on dealing with this unprecedented health emergency, adversarial states and cyber saboteurs have found an opportunity to crank up their offensive cyber operations. This is evident from the multiple attacks targeting critical national infrastructure engaged in fighting the pandemic, such as hospitals and other healthcare facilities and pharmaceutical companies. The absence of a global cyber security regime or agreed norms for state behaviour in cyber space has only complicated this scenario.

This introductory chapter will outline the lay of the land and identify the dynamics shaping the geopolitics of cyber space. It will then review the international community's efforts to create the ever-elusive rules-based order in cyber space.

Cyber space as an extension of geopolitical rivalries

On 8 December 2020, FireEye, an American cyber security firm, was the target of hacking by what it described as "a nation with top-tier offensive capabilities".[2] In the last few years, the firm has proactively tracked and publicised several Chinese and Russian cyber operations called Advanced Persistent Threats (APTs).[3] The hackers appeared to be interested in the details of the specific government customers of FireEye. They stole the company's internal hacking tools, used to test cyber security preparedness of its clients. This attack was followed by a series of breaches targeting the US government agencies, including Departments of Treasury, Commerce, Homeland Security's Cybersecurity and Infrastructure

DOI: 10.4324/9781003152910-1

Security Agency and the Energy Department's National Nuclear Security Administration.[4] Both FireEye and US officials have alleged that Russia was behind these breaches.[5,6] These consecutive attacks mark a significant escalation of geopolitical rivalry in cyber space. They are symbolic of the attacks taking place over the last few years, where nation-states have deployed advanced malware, utilised zero-day vulnerabilities and enlisted resourceful nationalistic hackers to target their adversaries' computer networks and critical infrastructure.

Since the attack on the Estonian computer networks in 2007, alleged to have been carried out by Russia-based hackers, such attacks have become the new normal in the cyber space. A review of the attacks which have happened since then amply demonstrates the inter-weaving of geopolitical rivalries with cyber warfare. The evolution of technology has enabled the proliferation of tools required for launching such penetrating attacks.

Table 1.1 lists some of the most significant cyber attacks since the attack in Estonia. As can be seen from the list, many of the attacks have targeted critical national infrastructure – from nuclear reactors, as happened during the Stuxnet virus attack, to banks and payment systems, as seen in the Bangladesh Bank's hacking in 2016. The problem of attribution has acted as a critical enabler for many of these attacks, since the attack is usually routed through multiple servers located in different countries. As a result, pinpointing the perpetrator of the attack is difficult. However, in recent years, utilising its technical skills and forensic capabilities, the United States has made significant progress in identifying people responsible for various cyber attacks – what is known as "naming and shaming". For instance, in 2018, the US Department of Justice charged the "Lazarus group", a North Korea-based hacking syndicate, as being responsible for multiple attacks, including the WannaCry Ransomware 2.0 attack, hacking of the Bangladesh Bank account and the targeting of Sony Corporation's servers.[7] Yet identifying the complicity of nation-states in such attacks has proved to be a generally difficult proposition.

However, the US actions have also helped to delineate another key trend – reliance on proxy non-state actors, such as hacktivists, hacking groups and organised cyber criminals to launch cyber attacks. This has effectively blurred the state/non-state actor distinction. It has also allowed the states to "circumvent attribution and the potential consequences involved".[8,9]

These surging cyber attacks have both security and business implications. The national security implications are evident from the Stuxnet virus' impact, which successfully disrupted the Iranian centrifuges, slowed down its reactors and upset Tehran's nuclear ambitions. The virus is widely believed to be a joint creation of the United States and Israel. These attacks' business implications can be seen from the disruptions of the critical business systems, as was observed during the outbreak of the 2017 NotPetya ransomware attack. The virus disrupted operations at many firms, including that of Maersk, the Danish shipping company. This disruption delayed the company's cargo container deliveries. This delay impacted the global supply chain, further disrupting manufacturing operations in many other countries.[10] More importantly, the example of the NotPetya attack also shows that

Table 1.1 Major cyber security incidents worldwide since 2007 (excluding India)

Year	Target	Incident	Implications
2007	Estonia	Distributed Denial of Service (DDoS) attacks against Estonian websites	The attack, suspected to have been carried out by Russia, disabled the government's websites, political parties, news organisations and banks. While it was not a significant attack in terms of the actual damage, it demonstrated the impact caused by disruptions of internet-enabled services. Since then, Estonia has invested heavily in strengthening its digital infrastructure.
2008	Georgia	DDoS attacks against Georgian computer networks	The Georgian government accused Russia of launching attacks against its computer networks when both countries were fighting to control the territory of South Ossetia. The attack disabled almost 90% of official Georgian websites.
2010	Iran	Discovery of Stuxnet virus targeting Iranian nuclear programme	Allegedly designed by the United States and Israel, the virus slowed down the Iranian nuclear reactor at Natanz, affecting the Iranian nuclear programme. It also impacted operations at critical infrastructure facilities and manufacturing sites in many other countries.
2011	Europe	Duqu virus hits European computer networks	The Duqu virus, similar to Stuxnet, targeted a specific number of organisations in Europe. It was used to steal information that could be utilised to attack the Industrial Control Systems.
2012	Saudi Aramco	Cyber attack against Saudi Aramco oil company	In retaliation for Stuxnet, Iranian hackers reportedly launched a massive cyber attack targeting Aramco, a Saudi Arabian government flagship. It erased critical corporate data from Aramco's 30,000 computers.
2013	Target Corporation	Credit card data breach at Target Corporation	The breach affected approximately 40 million consumers, forcing Target Corp to pay USD $18.5 million in the settlement.
2013-18	Worldwide	Malware attack targeting banks in Brazil, North America, Europe and Asia-Pacific	Carbanak, a cyber criminal gang primarily based in Europe, deployed malware in the systems of more than 100 banks, to steal upwards of USD $300 million – possibly as high as USD $1.1 billion. The malware imitated bank procedures by recording bank employees' computer activity.
2014	Sony Corporation	Data breach in the Sony Corporation's computer networks	Allegedly backed by the North Korean government, a group of hackers breached Sony Corporation's computers in the US, stealing sensitive data including confidential emails, business plans and employee details. The attack was reportedly in response to a satirical movie based on North Korean leader Kim Jong–Un, produced by Sony Pictures. The attack reportedly cost Sony more than USD $100 million to investigate, to repair or replace computers and to take measures to prevent future attacks.

(Continued)

Table 1.1 (Continued)

Year	Target	Incident	Implications
2014	North Korea	Suspected DDoS attack against North Korean computer networks	North Korea accused the United States of attacking its computer networks and shutting down the internet for many days. The attack was reportedly in response to the hacking of the Sony Corporation's computers.
2014	JPMorgan Chase	Data breach at American bank JPMorgan Chase	The attack resulted in the data of 83 million accounts being compromised.
2014	Mt. Gox Bitcoin exchange	Hackers target Mt. Gox Bitcoin exchange in Japan	In an attack which persisted for years, hackers stole from Mt. Gox 850,000 bitcoins worth USD $460 million – 7% of all bitcoins in circulation. Soon after it suspended trading and filed for bankruptcy.
2015	Office of Personnel Management	Data breach in the servers of the Office of Personnel Management	The attack, blamed on China by the US, resulted in 21.5 million former and prospective federal employees' data being stolen.
2015	Anthem Inc. insurance company	Data breach in the Anthem insurance company in the US	The breach exposed the records of approximately 78.8 million consumers. Investigations concluded the involvement of a foreign nation in the breach. The company was forced to pay USD $115 million to settle consumer claims.
2015	Banco del Austro, Ecuador-based bank	SWIFT credentials of Banco del Austro stolen by hackers	Unidentified hackers secured the bank employee's SWIFT logon credentials to steal USD $12 million. The breach was linked to the North Korea-affiliated Lazarus hacker group.
2016	Ukraine	DDoS attack against Ukrainian power companies	Suspected Russian hackers hacked into the three power companies' networks in Western Ukraine, which disrupted energy supplies in eight provinces, affecting more than 80,000 people.
2016	Bangladesh Bank	Hacking of Bangladesh Bank's account at Federal Reserve Bank, New York	Computer servers were hacked to issue instructions via SWIFT network for illegally transferring USD $951 million from the Bangladesh Bank's account in the Federal Reserve Bank. Transactions worth USD $101 million were successful. Bangladesh Bank has recovered USD $38 million so far. The attack has been linked to the Lazarus group.
2016	US election infrastructure	Targeting of the American election infrastructure during the 2016 presidential elections	Suspected Russia-based hackers scanned voter registration databases for vulnerabilities, attempted intrusions and, in some cases, successfully breached the database. This breach was accompanied by cyber attacks against the presidential campaign of Hillary Clinton and the Democratic National Committee.

Year	Target	Attack	Description
2017	Worldwide	'WannaCry' Ransomware attack	An exploit developed out of the intelligence gathering and hacking tools used by the US NSA quickly spread through computer networks to lockout computers in the critical infrastructure sector of many countries, including the financial sector.
2017	Worldwide	'Petya' and 'NotPetya' ransomware attack	Evolved versions of the 'WannaCry' ransomware targeted government and critical business systems. The attack hit Ukraine the hardest.
2017	Equifax	Data breach at Equifax credit monitoring agency in the US	Vulnerability in the company's computer network caused a data breach potentially impacting personal information relating to 143 million consumers in the United States, in addition to some consumers in the UK and Canada. Post-breach, the company lost more than USD $3 billion in stock market value.
2017	Deloitte	Data breach in Deloitte's email server	The breach compromised the firm's global email server, and may have accessed its clients' usernames, passwords and personal details. While the breach was discovered in March 2017, the attackers may have had access to Deloitte's systems since late 2016.
2019	United States	Targeting of multiple Microsoft email accounts	Phosphorus, a group affiliated with the Iranian government, targeted a US presidential campaign, host of serving and former government officials, journalists and prominent Iranians living outside Iran. Microsoft reported the malicious activity.
2020	FireEye	Data breach of FireEye cyber security firm	According to FireEye, "a nation with top-tier offensive capabilities" targeted the company to steal its internal hacking tools.
2020	US government	Malware attack on United States government agencies and private corporations	Suspected Russia-based hackers targeted multiple US government agencies, including Homeland Security and nuclear programmes, making it one of the largest breaches of US government agencies in history. The attack targeted private corporations as well, including Microsoft.

Source: Gateway House Research

businesses are getting caught up in these offensive cyber operations, sometimes as the target but most of the times as collateral damage or targets of opportunity. WannaCry malware, for instance, launched by North Korea, affected more than 200,000 computers in over 150 countries, including those of Boeing, FedEx, Hitachi, Renault etc. in 2017.[11] Similarly, the Stuxnet virus disrupted operations at manufacturing sites in many countries in 2010.

Combined with these penetrating cyber breaches are the foreign disinformation and cyber enabled-propaganda operations, which have assumed equally menacing proportions. Ironically, the very strength of the democratic societies – public debates, alternative viewpoints and free flow of information – seem to have contributed to the thriving of these disinformation campaigns. The threat posed by these foreign-directed propaganda campaigns was demonstrated during the 2016 American presidential elections, when Russia-linked entities allegedly targeted millions of American voters on Facebook.

The unrelenting cyber-enabled commercial espionage operations outdo these disruptive cyber attacks and disinformation campaign. Every state has traditionally carried out espionage, and it is an accepted part of statecraft worldwide. In a sense, states are both perpetrators and victims of this phenomenon. The proliferation of hacking tools and surveillance technology has catalysed cyber-enabled espionage and extended it to previously untapped domains, such as commercial and defence-industrial facilities. In 2013, documents leaked by a former employee of the National Security Agency (NSA), Edward Snowden, revealed the scale and extent of American surveillance activities, including spying on foreign companies such as Petrobras, Siemens and Huawei – direct competitors of several American businesses.[12] Snowden's revelations also showed that the NSA's PRISM surveillance programme worked closely with multiple tech majors such as Google, Yahoo and Microsoft to access millions of communication pieces.

For their part, the United States government agencies have disclosed how Chinese and Russian hackers have repeatedly breached America's and its allies' computer networks – both government and commercial. In October 2014, Mandiant cyber security firm revealed how Russian hackers targeted the American government and security establishment to glean information on various strategic issues.[13] Distinct from Russian cyber espionage are the Chinese efforts, which focus on economic gains through espionage. As an example of China's cyber-enabled commercial espionage, the United States has often cited Beijing's intellectual property theft of the F35 stealth fighter aircraft programme data. The US intelligence community has accused China of stealing the F35's design and radar modules data and incorporating it into its stealth fighter aircraft, the J20.[14] According to Washington, commercial espionage attempts like these have adversely affected the United States' economic fortunes and weakened innovation.[15]

Given the interdependent nature of economic ties with China, countries at the receiving end of China's espionage operations had been reluctant to attribute them to China. But this changed in 2013, when for the first time the US Department of Defense officially stated that the Chinese government was launching cyber attacks against the US.[16] This was followed by Canada in 2014, when the country's Chief

Information Officer blamed a "highly sophisticated Chinese state-sponsored actor" for breaching the National Research Council's computer systems.[17] This naming and shaming, however, seems to have made little difference to China.

Together, these developments have made cyber warfare a truly hybrid warfare phenomenon characterised by non-state actors' use as proxies, aggressive use of information tactics and plausible deniability.[18] This has dismantled the binary distinction between war and peace and created grey zones of conflicts.

Realising the tremendous impact of the internet and cyber space on the battlefield and military operations and as part of hybrid warfare, major military powers such as the United States, Russia and China had stayed ahead of the curve by establishing dedicated cyber entities within their militaries and intelligence setups.[19] For them, this was also the logical extension and upgrade of their espionage capabilities and propaganda operations. As geopolitical rivalries began spilling into cyber space, these entities took advantage of the attribution problem and demonstrated their offensive capabilities through repeated attacks targeting their adversaries.

Since the Estonian attack in 2007, national security establishments worldwide have debated if, when and in what manner states should respond militarily to a cyber attack. A related question has been if and when a cyber attack should be considered an "act of war", and when states should invoke the "right to self-defence" and deploy kinetic weapons. This became a particularly troubling concern as the number of, and disruptions caused by, cyber attacks surged, yet they did not reach the level of what can be considered equivalent to an "armed attack".

So far, states have mostly chosen to respond by launching retaliatory cyber attacks and hacking into their adversaries' systems. For instance, after the Stuxnet attack on the Iranian nuclear programme, Iranian government-linked hackers were suspected of hacking into Aramco, a Saudi Arabian government-owned oil company, in 2012, causing significant disruption.[20] However, with mounting cyber attacks, it appears that the states' threshold for military retaliation – at least towards the non-state actors – has lowered. In 2015, the United States killed an operative of the Daesh terrorist group in an airstrike in Syria, who had doxed about 1,300 American military personnel and government employees, by releasing their personally identifiable information online.[21] Most recently, in May 2019, the Israeli military pre-empted a cyber attack on its citizens from the Hamas terrorist group by bombing the group's technology division based in the Gaza Strip.[22] The Israeli action marked the first time that a military responded to a cyber threat on a real-time basis in a conflict situation, but it also sparked a debate on the military response's proportionality. These retaliatory cyber attacks and military responses have also fomented debates on norms for responsible state behaviour in cyber space.

Efforts to create a rules-based order in cyber space

A milestone in this process to shape such norms on responsible state behaviour was in 2004, when the United Nations (UN) set up the Group of Governmental Experts (GGE). However, that process ended without much progress, as divergences between the three major powers – the US, China and Russia – prevented any consensus on the agenda or the recommendations. The second GGE process was convened in 2009. Its report, submitted in 2010, recommended the need for the UN member states to expand confidence-building measures, which can reduce the risk of conflict in cyber space.[23] The next round of the GGE began in 2012, and its report in 2013 recognised the applicability of international law to cyber space – a significant headway in shaping the norms.[24] This process was taken forward by the GGE in 2014–2015, which recommended that states "should not conduct or knowingly support ICT activity that intentionally damages or otherwise impairs the use and operation of critical infrastructure".[25] This recommendation reflected the growing international concern about the security of critical infrastructure in the aftermath of the Stuxnet infections, which had infected many critical infrastructure facilities worldwide. However, the next GGE, convened in 2016, collapsed a year later due to disagreements between major powers over the applicability of specific international law principles for cyber space.[26]

Since then, the global momentum to shape norms for responsible state behaviour has become polarised, as evident in the creation of two parallel tracks at the UN in 2018 for discussion on this issue: the UN General Assembly voted to convene the next GGE for 2019–2021, and in parallel it also created a broader consultation process, termed the Open-Ended Working Group, which brought together "all interested states". In a sense, this was also the reflection of two competing visions for governing cyber space – one vision, spearheaded by Russia, emphasises the states' capacity to manage their cyber space effectively. In contrast, the other vision, championed by the United States, underlines the need to protect cyber space through international legal principles.

While states have accepted the need to collaborate to tackle the emerging cyber threats, just like other pressing global issues such as climate change or terrorism, they have found it difficult to make that intention materialise. As a result, even a basic global cyber security agreement or consensus on cyber security still eludes the international community. Much of the focus on cyber security issues has rightly shifted to bilateral agreements, such as the one between the United States and China when they signed a landmark agreement to limit their cyber-enabled espionage in September 2015.[27] The agreement ensured a momentary ceasefire in the bilateral cyber hostilities, but petered out after a few years. Nonetheless, it demonstrated the benefit of engaging bilaterally to resolve the problem, rather than getting stuck for years in a multilateral format. Indeed, states have found it much easier to proceed on these issues bilaterally with like-minded partners. As will be discussed in Chapter 6, India has adopted the same approach in its cyber diplomacy by strengthening cooperation with countries such as the United States, France and Australia.

While major powers have disagreed on how international law applies to cyber space, Europe has gone ahead in taking some steps to create an order in cyber space. At the heart of this process is Estonia, which was the first country to bear the brunt of geopolitical rivalries in cyber space. Since the 2007 attack, Estonia has strengthened its cyber defences. It is also home to the North Atlantic Treaty Organization's Cooperative Cyber Defence Centre of Excellence, set up just a few months after the Russia-engineered attack. This centre has also been at the forefront to illustrate international law's applicability to cyber space, through the much-acclaimed Tallinn Manual.[28] The document, drafted by a team of legal experts, is a collection of legal opinions for the states to apply international law to defend themselves from the cyber attacks, particularly those which can be considered "an armed attack". Europe has also taken the lead on another front, in the form of a Council of Europe's Budapest Convention on Cybercrime, 2001.[29] The Convention has attempted to evolve a common strategy for dealing with cyber crimes, including investigations, though China and India have opposed this agreement.

As noted earlier, businesses are also getting dragged into this geopolitical rivalry. As a result, businesses, mainly the technology majors, have realised their critical role in the evolving cyber security scenario, and are calling on stakeholders to introspect and think of ways to evolve a global cyber security framework. As the owner of the one of the most widely used proprietary softwares, Microsoft has been in the lead of calling on other stakeholders to work towards a regime. In 2017 when the WannaCry ransomware – traced to stolen hacking tools from the United States' NSA and which exploited a security vulnerability in Microsoft's Windows Operating System – infected computers around the world, Microsoft pointed out the dangers of security agencies "stockpiling of vulnerabilities" which can cause widespread damage.[30] It then called on states to adopt a responsible approach and consider the consequences of their actions in cyber space, just as they would do while using weapons in the physical world.

Just months before the WannaCry outbreak, Microsoft had proposed a "Digital Geneva Convention" which urged the governments and other stakeholders to protect "the public from nation-state threats in cyberspace".[31] The convention, among other things, proposed a commitment from states to not target technology companies, private sector or critical infrastructure. It also called on states to limit offensive cyber operations to avoid creating large-scale damage.[32] In 2018, the company took two initiatives: Tech Accords and Paris Call, which it hoped would shape cyber security cooperation in the tech domain.[33,34] The company reiterated its call for such a convention in the aftermath of the large-scale breach of the United States government agencies and hacking at FireEye, terming these attacks a "moment of reckoning".[35]

Finally, in the true spirit of the multi-stakeholder character of cyber space, global civil society has also played its part in shaping the debate on norms creation. Initiatives such as the Global Commission on the Stability of Cyberspace and Global Commission on Internet Governance have tried to develop core fundamentals for responsible state behaviour by working with politicians, former diplomats, academia, digital rights activists and lawyers.[36,37] Another notable effort was from the United Nations Secretary General's Office, which set up a High-level Panel on Digital Cooperation, which can be termed a UN-sponsored civil society effort to examine how the UN can shape the debate in this space.[38]

The above overview reveals no dearth of initiatives to bring some semblance of order to the highly contested cyber space. The flurry of initiatives has led some analysts to term these an "incipient stage" of looking for cyber norms.[39] However, just like in other domains of international security, power and capabilities matter.

Therefore, how many of these initiatives succeed ultimately depends on what the three leading powers – the United States, Russia and China – decide. Indeed, these states, along with many others, have benefitted from cyber warfare and the absence of a clearly defined rules-based order. Accordingly, whether and how much these states are willing to cede space for other states and private sector entities to have a say will determine the shaping of cyber norms. Other powers such as India, Canada, Australia and the European Union are also essential in this process through their cyber diplomacy efforts.

Conclusion

The overview provided in this chapter makes it clear that internet and cyber space are no longer the democratisers, at least not in the manner in which they were previously perceived to be. Today, they have assumed an altogether different character, thanks to the prevalent major power tensions. Power politics notwithstanding, it will be imperative for the major powers to establish a modicum of understanding to restrain their geopolitical rivalries, given the implications of cyber space instability for international security. For instance, a consensus to not attack each other's critical infrastructure can undoubtedly act as a much-needed confidence-building measure. If such a measure is sustained for a reasonable amount of time, it can indeed lay the basis for creating a rules-based order. In the current fluid times, such an idea may appear idealistic, but the history of arms control agreements has demonstrated that only times of instability and escalated hostilities act as catalysts for major power cooperation.

Notes

1 "COVID-19 Cyberthreats," Interpol, accessed December 29, 2020, www.interpol.int/en/Crimes/Cybercrime/COVID-19-cyberthreats.
2 Kevin Mandia, "FireEye Shares Details of Recent Cyber Attack, Actions to Protect Community," *FireEye*, December 8, 2020, www.fireeye.com/blog/products-and-services/2020/12/fireeye-shares-details-of-recent-cyber-attack-actions-to-protect-community.html.
3 Shane Harris, *@War: The Rise of the Military-Internet Complex* (New York: Houghton Mifflin Harcourt, 2014), 210.
4 Hollie McKay, "Russia's Suspected Hacking Operation Targeted 5 US Agencies, 18K Entities," *Fox News*, December 16, 2020, www.foxnews.com/tech/foreign-hacking-public-private-entities-breached.
5 Brian Fung and Alex Marquardt, "US Agencies Investigating Hacking of Government Networks," *CNN*, December 14, 2020, https://edition.cnn.com/2020/12/13/politics/us-agencies-investigating-hacking-data-breach/index.html.
6 William Turton, Michael Riley and Jennifer Jacobs, "Hackers Tied to Russia Hit Nuclear Agency: Microsoft Is Exposed," *Bloomberg*, December 18, 2020, www.bloomberg.com/news/articles/2020-12-17/u-s-states-were-also-hacked-in-suspected-russian-attack.
7 "North Korean Regime-Backed Programmer Charged With Conspiracy to Conduct Multiple Cyber Attacks and Intrusions," Federal Bureau of Investigation, accessed December 29, 2020, www.justice.gov/opa/pr/north-korean-regime-backed-programmer-charged-conspiracy-conduct-multiple-cyber-attacks-and.

8 Sico van der Meer, "How States Could Respond to Non-State Cyber-Attackers," Clingendael Policy Brief, June 2020, www.clingendael.org/sites/default/files/2020-06/Policy_Brief_Cyber_non-state_June_2020.pdf.
9 Tim Maurer, *Cyber Mercenaries: The State, Hackers, and Power* (Cambridge: Cambridge University Press, 2018), 22.
10 Jacob Gronholt-Pedersen, "Maersk Says Global IT Breakdown Caused by Cyber Attack," *Reuters*, June 27, 2017, www.reuters.com/article/us-cyber-attack-maersk-idUSKBN19I1NO.
11 Dominic Gates, "Boeing Hit by WannaCry Virus, But Says Attack Caused Little Damage," *The Seattle Times*, March 28, 2018, www.seattletimes.com/business/boeing-aerospace/boeing-hit-by-wannacry-virus-fears-it-could-cripple-some-jet-production/.
12 Adam Segal, *The Hacked World Order* (New York: PublicAffairs, 2016), 119–125.
13 "Russia's APT28 Strategically Evolves Its Cyber Operations," FireEye, www.fireeye.com/current-threats/apt-groups/rpt-apt28.html.
14 Jeff Daniels, "Chinese Theft of Sensitive US Military Technology Is Still a 'Huge Problem,' Says Defense Analyst," *CNBC*, November 8, 2017, www.cnbc.com/2017/11/08/chinese-theft-of-sensitive-us-military-technology-still-huge-problem.html.
15 William C. Hannas, James Mulvenon and Anna B. Puglist, *Chinese Industrial Espionage: Technology Acquisitions and Military Modernization* (London: Routledge, 2013), 221.
16 "Annual Report to Congress: Military and Security Developments Involving the People's Republic of China 2013," United States Department of Defense, https://media.npr.org/documents/2013/may/2013%20China%20Report%20FINAL.pdf., 36.
17 Rosemary Barton, "Chinese Cyberattack Hits Canada's National Research Council," *CBC News*, July 29, 2014, www.cbc.ca/news/politics/chinese-cyberattack-hits-canada-s-national-research-council-1.2721241.
18 Sameer Patil, "Deterring the Hybrid Threat," *Gateway House*, December 6, 2017, www.gatewayhouse.in/debatingsecurityplus_excerpt/.
19 For U.S. Cyber Command, see Harris, *op. cit.*, 47–48.
20 Christopher Bronk and Eneken Tikk-Ringas, "The Cyber Attack on Saudi Aramco," *Survival* 55, no. 2 (April–May 2013): 81–96.
21 Terri Moon Cronk, "Iraq Progresses in ISIL Fight, Key Extremist Confirmed Dead," *DoD News*, August 28, 2015, www.defense.gov/Explore/News/Article/Article/615305/iraq-progresses-in-isil-fight-key-extremist-confirmed-dead/.
22 Israel Defense Forces (@IDF), "CLEARED FOR RELEASE: We Thwarted an Attempted Hamas Cyber Offensive Against Israeli Targets: Following Our Successful Cyber Defensive Operation, We Targeted a Building Where the Hamas Cyber Operatives Work. HamasCyberHQ.exe Has Been Removed," Twitter Tweet, May 5, 2019, https://twitter.com/IDF/status/1125066395010699264.
23 "Group of Governmental Experts on Developments in the Field of Information and Telecommunications in the Context of International Security," United Nations General Assembly, accessed December 29, 2020, https://undocs.org/A/65/201.
24 "Group of Governmental Experts on Developments in the Field of Information and Telecommunications in the Context of International Security," United Nations General Assembly, accessed December 29, 2020, www.unidir.org/files/medias/pdfs/developments-in-the-field-of-information-and-telecommunications-in-the-context-of-international-security-2012–2013-a-68–98-eng-0–518.pdf.
25 "Group of Governmental Experts on Developments in the Field of Information and Telecommunications in the Context of International Security," United Nations General Assembly, accessed December 29, 2020, www.un.org/ga/search/view_doc.asp?symbol=A/70/174.
26 Adam Segal, "The Development of Cyber Norms at the United Nations Ends in Deadlock: Now What?," *Council on Foreign Relations*, June 29, 2017, www.cfr.org/blog/development-cyber-norms-united-nations-ends-deadlock-now-what.

27 Sameer Patil, "US-China: No More Spy Games?," *The Diplomat*, October 29, 2015, https://thediplomat.com/2015/10/us-china-no-more-spy-games/.
28 Michael N. Schmitt (ed.), *Tallinn Manual 2.0 on the International Law Applicable to Cyber Operations* (Cambridge: Cambridge University Press, 2017).
29 Joseph S. Nye, "The Regime Complex for Managing Global Cyber Activities," Global Commission on Internet Governance Paper Series No. 1, May 2014, www.cigionline.org/sites/default/files/gcig_paper_no1.pdf, 6.
30 Brad Smith, "The Need for Urgent Collective Action to Keep People Safe Online: Lessons from Last Week's Cyberattack'," *Microsoft*, May 14, 2017, https://blogs.microsoft.com/on-the-issues/2017/05/14/need-urgent-collective-action-keep-people-safe-online-lessons-last-weeks-cyberattack/.
31 "A Digital Geneva Convention to Protect Cyberspace," Microsoft Policy Papers, accessed December 29, 2020, https://query.prod.cms.rt.microsoft.com/cms/api/am/binary/RW67QH.
32 Brad Smith, "The Need for a Digital Geneva Convention," *Microsoft*, February 14, 2017, https://blogs.microsoft.com/on-the-issues/2017/02/14/need-digital-geneva-convention/.
33 Brad Smith, "34 Companies Stand Up for Cybersecurity with a Tech Accord," *Microsoft*, April 17, 2018, https://blogs.microsoft.com/on-the-issues/2018/04/17/34-companies-stand-up-for-cybersecurity-with-a-tech-accord/.
34 "Paris Call for Trust and Security in Cyberspace," accessed December 29, 2020, https://pariscall.international/en/call.
35 Brad Smith, "A Moment of Reckoning: The Need for a Strong and Global Cybersecurity Response," *Microsoft*, December 17, 2020, https://blogs.microsoft.com/on-the-issues/2020/12/17/cyberattacks-cybersecurity-solarwinds-fireeye/.
36 "About," Global Commission on the Stability of Cyberspace, accessed December 29, 2020, https://cyberstability.org/about/.
37 "Global Commission on Internet Governance," Centre for International Governance Innovation, accessed December 29, 2020, www.cigionline.org/activity/global-commission-internet-governance.
38 "United Nations Secretary-General Appoints High-Level Panel on Digital Cooperation," United Nations, July 12, 2018, www.un.org/en/pdfs/HLP-on-Digital-Cooperation_Press-Release.pdf.
39 Syed Akbaruddin, "A Quest for Order Amid Cyber Insecurity," *The Hindu*, July 30, 2020, www.thehindu.com/opinion/lead/a-quest-for-order-amid-cyber-insecurity/article32225383.ece.

2 India's cyber security landscape
Vulnerabilities and responses

Introduction

With approximately 700 million users, India constitutes the second largest internet user base in the world, after China. The digital domain in India has undergone massive expansion since the introduction of internet services in India through the Education and Research Network (ERNET) project in 1986. Funded by the UN Development Programme and implemented by the Department of Electronics (the predecessor of the Ministry of Electronics and Information Technology – MEITY), the ERNET project connected different Indian academic institutions.[1] It was gradually expanded in the 1990s to provide internet services to ordinary Indians. This expansion of the internet spawned the growth of Information Technology (IT)-enabled services, making India an IT hub. This development was joined with the gradual adoption of IT by the Indian government. The arrival of social media platforms in the late 2000s added another dimension to this story of India's digital transformation.[2]

This chapter takes a broad overview of India's cyber security landscape by examining threats to India's computer networks, and steps taken by the stakeholders – government, regulators and the private sector – to tackle these threats. Subsequent chapters examine some of these issues in detail.

Overview of threats to India's cyber space

The rapid proliferation of the internet and the expansion of the user base in India also saw an accompanying rise in cyber crimes. First-time internet users, along with their poor cyber hygiene habits, meant that Indians became easy victims of social engineering tactics and online advance-fee scams.[3] One such scam, which became particularly notorious in duping hundreds of Indian internet users, was the Nigerian phishing scam emails, where victims were lured into making advance payment to the scamsters, in return for a larger payment afterwards.[4] As per one study, in 2013, Indians lost USD $870 million to this fraud, which made India one of the top five growing markets for such fraud.[5] There was also a rise in cyber attacks on Indian computer networks. The most common type initially was hacking of Indian websites, mostly government ones, by Pakistan or China-based hackers in "tit for tat" attacks. However, soon these nuisance value attacks evolved to become advanced and targeted.

DOI: 10.4324/9781003152910-2

Technical data from the Indian Computer Emergency Response Team (CERT-IN) reveals the exponential increase in cases of cyber incidents in India – from a mere 552 cases in 2006 (the earliest year the data is available) to 394,499 cases in 2019 – as can be seen in Figure 2.1.[6] These include cases of malware attacks, DDoS attacks, website defacement etc. proving that attacks on Indian computer networks have grown in scale and impact.

As Table 2.1 shows, India's government computer networks and commercial servers have witnessed multiple data breaches, espionage attempts and malware attacks. The most prominent instance of cyber-enabled commercial espionage on Indian computer networks was the APT30 operation, carried out by a China-based group, which was most likely state-sponsored.[7] According to FireEye, which monitors offensive Chinese cyber operations, the APT30 espionage operation ran for a decade – it was discovered in 2015. It harvested information from Indian computer networks on geopolitical issues relevant to the Chinese Communist Party, such as the India-China border dispute, Indian naval activity in the South China Sea and India's relations with its South Asian neighbours.

Concerns about implications of cyber attacks were amplified in 2010, after the Stuxnet malware infected multiple computer networks running on the Supervisory Control and Data Acquisition (SCADA)/Industrial Control Systems in India. There was no major disruption, unlike the Iranian nuclear programme (which was the target of the Stuxnet). Nonetheless, these disruptions brought to fore the issue of critical infrastructure protection and the vulnerability that spanned government and private sectors, as both operated facilities in critical sectors such as communications, power plants and oil pipelines.

Apart from government networks, the financial sector also remains a significant target for hackers. In the most serious incident of a data breach so far, a malware attack hit the India-based servers of Hitachi Payment Systems, which enabled unauthorised access to Indian debit card data. This breach forced 19 Indian banks

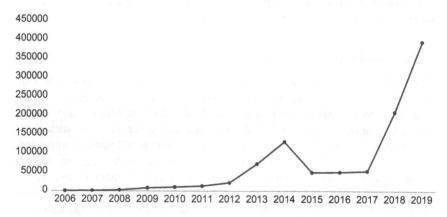

Figure 2.1 Cyber security incidents in India (2006–2019)

Source: Data compiled from the Indian Computer Emergency Response Team

Table 2.1 Major cyber security incidents involving Indian computer networks

Year	Incident	Implications
2010	Stuxnet infections of Indian computer systems	Part of a global attack, the malware infected computer systems across India, including computer systems at power plants and oil pipelines in Gujarat and Haryana. No other significant disruption was reported.
2015	Foreign espionage operation focused on government and commercial computer networks	A decade-long espionage operation through the APT30 vector, carried out by a China-based group that was most likely state-sponsored. The data harvested was political, economic and military. The APT30 utilised the same tools, tactics and infrastructure for ten years, exposing a major vulnerability in critical computer networks.
2016	DCNS data breach	Designs and data on India's Kalvari-class submarines, along with those of Malaysia and Chile, were leaked from the French shipbuilder DCNS, which was involved in submarine-building projects. The breach reportedly revealed confidential stealth capabilities of submarines. Commercial rivalry was suspected to be behind the data breach.
2016	Breach in Union Bank of India's foreign exchange account	Successful phishing attack activated malware that gave hackers access to payment-processing codes that were used to steal USD $170 million. The timely intervention resulted in retrieving the entire amount.
2016	Malware attack on the Hitachi Payment Systems	Malware compromised the payment infrastructure, resulting in the data breach of approximately 3.2 million debit cards. This was the biggest data breach in the Indian history, resulting in losses totalling Rs. 1.3 crore.
2017	Bank of Maharashtra fraud	Fraudsters exploited a software vulnerability in the bank application for an unauthorised fund transfer. This caused the Bank of Maharashtra a loss of Rs. 25 crores, which was partially recovered.
2017	'WannaCry' and 'Petya' ransomware attacks	Part of the global attack, the 'WannaCry' ransomware affected many government and commercial systems in India, but not many infections were officially reported. Some estimates put the number of infections at 48,000 computers. The Petya ransomware attack most prominently hit the container terminals of APM Terminals Mumbai, at India's biggest container port, the Jawaharlal Nehru Port Trust.
2018	Breach at City Union Bank	Cyber criminals hacked into the bank's payment systems to steal USD $2 million. The bank managed to retrieve USD $1 million.
2018	Cosmos Bank fraud	The bank lost Rs. 94 crores due to a malware attack that authorised fraudulent transactions, with ATM withdrawals being reportedly made in 28 countries.
2019	Malware attack on Kudankulam nuclear reactor	The attack breached the reactor's administrative network, but no major disruption was reported.

(Continued)

Table 2.1 (Continued)

Year	Incident	Implications
2020	Dr. Reddy's Laboratories data breach	The breach temporarily forced the pharmaceutical company to cease its operations at manufacturing plants worldwide. It also isolated its data centre services to maintain the integrity of the data.
2020	Press Trust of India ransomware attack	The attack on the news agency's computer servers disrupted its operations and affected news delivery services to its subscribers.

Source: Gateway House research, based on official data and media reports

to replace 3.2 million debit cards.[8] In between these high-profile attacks, periodic attacks targeting various organisations and businesses have continued, as evident from the CERT-IN's annual reports.[9] India has yet to attribute a cyber attack to any state or non-state actor publicly, although privately, officials do point out the involvement of China and Pakistan in many of these attacks.

One significant dimension of the cyber threat which Table 2.1 doesn't cover is the use of cyber space by terrorist groups. Pakistan-based anti-India terrorist groups, such as the Lashkar-e-Taiba and Jaish-e-Mohammed, have used cyber space and social media platforms primarily for radicalisation, propaganda and recruitment.[10] However, as the example of the Daesh terrorist group has shown, cyber space is also being used for mobilising "lone wolves" to execute terrorist attacks. Encryption technologies such as The Onion Router (TOR) are aiding these nefarious activities. Moreover, the digital black markets or dark net marketplaces hosted on TOR have acted as a force multiplier for illicit activities, such as drug trafficking and sale of other contraband. As will be noted in Chapter 5, these marketplaces have thrived, despite regular crackdowns by the law enforcement agencies.

Cyber security policy push in the last decade

In response to persistent cyber threats, India has stepped up its cyber security focus by creating an extensive institutional and regulatory framework in the last decade. The highlight of this is the IT Act 2000 (amended in 2008) and the National Cyber Security Policy (NCSP) of 2013. Keeping up with constant changes in cyber space, the NCSP is now being updated and recast as the National Cyber Security Strategy. In 2015, the government created the post of the National Cyber Security Coordinator (NCSC) within the National Security Council Secretariat (NSCS), to synchronise efforts on cyber security issues at the national level and coordinate between the relevant government agencies. The advisor reports directly to the National Security Advisor within the Prime Minister's Office.

Apart from the NCSC, at present, cyber security issues are handled by different ministries at technical (MEITY), financial (Ministry of Finance-MoF), security (Ministry of Home Affairs-MHA) and defence (Ministry of Defence-MoD) levels (see Figure 2.2).

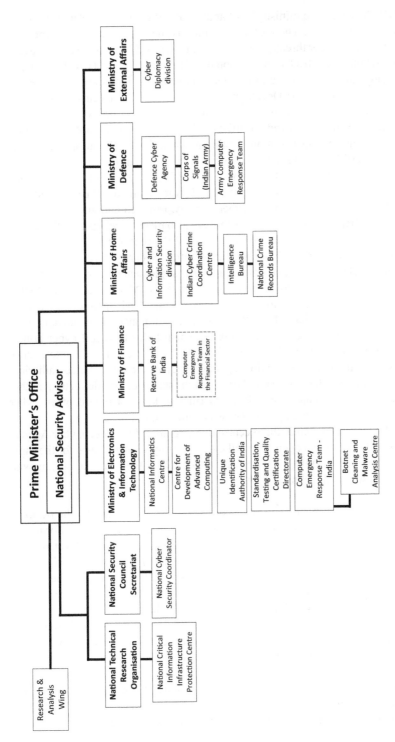

Figure 2.2 India's cyber security architecture

Source: Gateway House Research

- **MEITY**: as a "line ministry", it handles all policy matters relating to information technology. The CERT-IN, which is the nodal technical agency for dealing with cyber threats, is located within the MEITY. Other relevant agencies within the MEITY are National Informatics Centre (which primarily develops and maintains e-governance applications, including official email addresses), Centre for Development of Advanced Computing (C-DAC for research and development in IT, electronics and other areas), Unique Identification Authority of India (UIDAI, which collects and manages the Aadhar data) and Standardisation, Testing and Quality Certification Directorate (which certifies software and hardware for use in India);
- **MoF**: within the MoF, the Reserve Bank of India (RBI) set up in 2017 the Reserve Bank Information Technology Private Limited (ReBIT) to address its IT requirements including cyber security, research and audit and assessment of RBI-regulated entities. There are also plans to set up a CERT for the financial sector, as announced in the 2017–2018 central budget;[11]
- **MHA**: the ministry's Cyber and Information Security division deals with matters relating to cyber crimes and the implementation of the National Information Security Policy and Guidelines.[12] The MHA operates the Indian Cyber Crime Coordination Centre (I4C) – the lead agency for tackling cyber crimes in India.[13] The I4C has various component units, including the National Cybercrime Reporting portal, which helps to report cyber crimes against women and children. Apart from the I4C, there is also the Intelligence Bureau, which, as the principal agency for domestic intelligence-gathering, also monitors cyber space regularly, though that is not its sole focus. Another agency, the National Crime Records Bureau, keeps a record of all cyber crimes and incidents as part of crimes committed in India;
- **MoD**: within the MoD, the recently operationalised Defence Cyber Agency acts as the principal agency for all cyber security-related issues for the three services and the MoD.[14] There is also the CERT for the Army for dealing with cyber issues at a technical level.

Besides these four ministries, cyber security issues are addressed by the National Technical Research Organisation (NTRO) and National Critical Information Infrastructure Protection Centre (NCIIPC, a nodal body under the NTRO, responsible for securing India's critical national infrastructure). Separately, the Research and Analysis Wing also monitors cyber space, especially the foreign cyber operations against India, within its overall mandate of gathering external intelligence. The Ministry of External Affairs (MEA)'s Cyber Diplomacy division, meanwhile, projects these domestic initiatives and India's positions on cyber and digital issues at the international level and multilateral fora in coordination with the MEITY.

At the state level, the approach to cyber security issues varies from state to state. Some, such as Maharashtra and Kerala, have attempted to carve out a distinct focus on cyber issues through projects such as "Maharashtra Cyber"[15] and "Cyberdome",[16] respectively. In contrast, most other states have tackled cyber issues within the IT department or division. Also, state police forces have set up separate units, variously known as state cyber crime cell, cyber crime labs, cyber crime branch, cyber police stations, social media labs etc. to deal with cyber security and related issues.

The broad policy guidelines set by the IT Act 2000 and the NCSP 2013 are translated into multiple specific guidelines, advisories, technical frameworks and standards from many government bodies and departments, such as the CERT-IN and the RBI. These have sought to regulate many dimensions of cyber space, such as critical infrastructure, digital payments, fintech, malware attacks etc. Additionally, the government is planning to bring in legislation governing personal and non-personal data, as well as Intermediary Guidelines to regulate social media platforms.[17,18] The Indian government is also engaged in capacity-building of law enforcement agencies through awareness-raising, training programmes and enhancing cyber forensics skills. However, much more needs to be done, particularly on cyber hygiene and forensics, given the magnitude of the cyber threats.

In addition to the previous points, to counter indoctrination and the use of cyber space by terrorist groups, India has set up Central Monitoring System (CMS), a surveillance tool to keep a tab on suspicious communications, under the aegis of the Intelligence Bureau.[19] However, many civil society organisations and cyber analysts have expressed concerns over the CMS' expansive reach and its privacy implications.[20,21] The absence of comprehensive privacy legislation which can set limits on state surveillance in India further complicates this issue.[22]

Major challenges

The account in the previous section demonstrates that in response to the expanding cyber threat landscape, India has treated cyber security as a core national interest and, therefore, a policy priority. It has created an extensive institutional architecture to tackle cyber threats. However, multiple challenges are afflicting India's response. One of the significant challenges is the fragmented approach of government agencies. The NCSC was supposed to bridge this fragmented approach and achieve coordination between different agencies. But five years since the appointment, the NCSC has to do without an overarching empowered institution which can enable him to perform his tasks optimally. His role is also stymied by the turf battles between bureaucrats, security and technical agencies, as with other areas of national security decision-making. Moreover, while this setup has attempted to work with the private sector, industry, particularly the banking and financial sector, has often complained of inadequate to almost absent coordination on cyber security issues.

In mitigating cyber threats, law enforcement agencies also face the challenge of inadequate cyber forensics, which critically impairs cyber crime investigations. This is particularly so in case of advanced cyber crimes such as data breach and hacking, in tier two and three cities. Consequently, only a fraction of cyber crime incidents is reported and registered in India. The lack of capacity is reflected in the lower conviction rate for cyber crimes – in 2019, convictions happened in only 366 cases – with an even greater number of cases pending with the police and judiciary.[23]

Additionally, this inadequate capacity also shapes perceptions of the private sector in terms of incident reporting to law enforcement agencies and regulators. This was evident in many companies' reluctance to report infections of the WannaCry ransomware attack in May 2017. In a temporary measure to overcome inadequate capacity, police departments in many states have engaged the services of private cyber security consultants for investigations.

Another major challenge from the government and industry perspective is the poor cyber hygiene of Indian internet users. As will be discussed in Chapter 4, internet users' lack of awareness about safe online behaviour, along with cyber threats in general, adversely affects cyber security, particularly in the digital payment systems space, where expanded use of mobile banking and wallets has also led to a surge in cyber crimes.

An even more significant handicap when it comes to cyber crimes is the transnational nature of the crime, spanning multiple jurisdictions. Despite the best intentions of the law and order machinery, it is difficult to work with other countries to tackle cyber crimes – information exchanges on criminal activities are time-consuming, and legal practices vary, despite having mutual legal assistance treaties with like-minded countries.[24]

Conclusion

Being located in a hostile regional environment, India's cyber threat landscape is vast and varied, mainly due to the ability and capacity of cyber saboteurs to think and act across multiple jurisdictions, which remain unchallenged in no small measure. Subsequent chapters will examine in detail three pressing cyber security challenges – protecting critical infrastructure, securing digital payment systems and the emerging threat of the 'deep web'. These chapters will also review policy measures taken by Indian policy makers in these domains. In addition to domestic initiatives, in recent years, India has also stepped up its diplomacy to work with like-minded countries in countering cyber threats. Chapter 6 will illustrate India's lead in cyber diplomacy to shape norms for global cyber order.

Notes

1 Srinivasan Ramani, "Bringing the Internet to India," in *netCh@kra: 15 Years of Internet in India, Retrospect and Roadmaps*, eds. Madanmohan Rao and Osama Manzar (New Delhi: Digital Empowerment Foundation, 2011), 47–62.
2 Preeti Mahajan, "Use of Social Networking in a Linguistically and Culturally Rich India," *The International Information & Library Review* 41, no. 3 (2009): 129–136.
3 According to the United States Federal Bureau of Investigation, an advance-fee scam occurs when "the victim pays money to someone in anticipation of receiving something of greater value – such as a loan, contract, investment, or gift – and then receives little or nothing in return." See "Advance Fee Schemes," Federal Bureau of Investigation, accessed August 19, 2020, www.fbi.gov/scams-and-safety/common-scams-and-crimes/advance-fee-schemes.
4 Chi Luu, "The Life Changing Linguistics of . . . Nigerian Scam Emails," *Jstor Daily*, September 11, 2019, https://daily.jstor.org/the-life-changing-linguistics-of-nigerian-scam-emails/.

5 "419 Advance Fee Fraud Statistics 2013," Ultrascan Advanced Global Investigations, accessed March 12, 2020, www.ultrascan-agi.com/public_html/html/pdf_files/Pre-Release-419_Advance_Fee_Fraud_Statistics_2013-July-10-2014-NOT-FINAL-1.pdf.
6 "Annual Report," Indian Computer Emergency Response Team, accessed August 19, 2020, www.cert-in.org.in/.
7 "Threat Research: APT 30 and the Mechanics of a Long-Running Cyber Espionage Operation," Fireeye, accessed June 15, 2020, www2.fireeye.com/rs/fireye/images/rpt-apt30.pdf.
8 "Statement Pertaining to Press Reports on Debit Card Compromise," National Payments Corporation of India, accessed June 15, 2019, www.npci.org.in/sites/default/files/Statementpertainingtopressreportsondebitcardcompromise.pdf.
9 "2019 Annual Report," Indian Computer Emergency Response Team, accessed August 19, 2020, www.cert-in.org.in/.
10 Prabha Rao, "Online Radicalisation: The Example of Burhan Wani," *Manohar Parrikar Institute for Defence Studies and Analyses*, July 16, 2016, https://idsa.in/issuebrief/online-radicalisation-burhan-wani_prao_160716.
11 "Report of the Working Group for setting up of Computer Emergency Response Team in the financial sector (CERT-Fin)," Department of Economic Affairs, Ministry of Finance, accessed June 15, 2010, http://dea.gov.in/sites/default/files/Press-CERT-Fin%20Report.pdf.
12 "Cyber and Information Security (C&IS) Division," Ministry of Home Affairs, accessed August 19, 2020, www.mha.gov.in/division_of_mha/cyber-and-information-security-cis-division.
13 "Details about Indian Cybercrime Coordination Centre (I4C) Scheme," Ministry of Home Affairs, accessed August 19, 2020, www.mha.gov.in/division_of_mha/cyber-and-information-security-cis-division/Details-about-Indian-Cybercrime-Coordination-Centre-I4C-Scheme.
14 "Raksha Mantri Reviews Defence Cooperation Mechanism," Press Information Bureau, accessed August 19, 2020, https://pib.gov.in/Pressreleaseshare.aspx?PRID=1573610.
15 "Who Are We?," Maharashtra Cyber, accessed June 15, 2020, www.mhcyber.gov.in/who-are-we.php.
16 "Welcome to Cyberdome," Kerala Police Cyberdome, accessed August 19, 2020, www.cyberdome.kerala.gov.in/.
17 Ambika Khanna, "Re-Assessing India's Non-Personal Data," *Gateway House*, October 20, 2020, www.gatewayhouse.in/indias-non-personal-data/.
18 Ambika Khanna, "India's Evolving Fintech Laws," *Gateway House*, March 14, 2019, www.gatewayhouse.in/indias-fintech-laws/.
19 "Amendment to the Unified License Agreement Regarding Central Monitoring System," Department of Telecom, accessed August 19, 2020, https://dot.gov.in/sites/default/files/DOC231013.pdf?download=1.
20 "Watch the Watchmen Series Part 2: The Centralised Monitoring System," Internet Freedom Foundation, accessed August 19, 2020, https://internetfreedom.in/watch-the-watchmen-series-part-2-the-centralised-monitoring-system/.
21 Jaideep Reddy, "The Central Monitoring System and Privacy: Analysing What We Know So Far," *Indian Journal of Law and Technology* 10 (2014): 41–62.
22 Sameer Patil, "Policy Catalyst: India's Privacy Law," *Gateway House*, June 13, 2014, www.gatewayhouse.in/policy-catalyst-crafting-indias-privacy-law/.
23 "Crime in India, 2019," National Crime Records Bureau, Ministry of Home Affairs, accessed June 15, 2020, https://ncrb.gov.in/sites/default/files/CII%202019%20Volume%202.pdf.
24 Indian Police Service Officers, Interview by Sameer Patil, June 2017.

3 Protecting India's critical infrastructure

Introduction

India is aiming to become a USD $1 trillion digital economy by 2025.[1] Undergirding this ambitious goal is the security and uninterrupted functioning of the nation's critical infrastructure and critical business systems, such as telecommunication networks, financial systems, power grids, oil pipelines and nuclear reactors. The 2010 Stuxnet virus attack demonstrated for the first time the worldwide vulnerability of the computer networks responsible for protecting this critical infrastructure. The virus not only targeted the Iranian nuclear programme – its ultimate target – but also exposed vulnerabilities of other systems through which it travelled to reach that reactor.[2] Since then, protecting the nation's critical infrastructure has emerged as a significant cyber security concern for the Indian government.

India's critical infrastructure vulnerabilities span public as well as private sectors. The major vulnerability arises out of the obsolete SCADA software systems, which are used to manage operations at critical infrastructure facilities. In recent years, India has attempted to plug these vulnerabilities through several policy measures. It has also set up a specialised government agency which works with the private sector to manage this threat. This chapter examines the cyber threats to India's critical infrastructure, the emerging concern about securing election infrastructure and measures implemented by the government and industry to protect their computer networks.

Defining critical national infrastructure

Critical infrastructure is that infrastructure which provides essential services. These services are the backbone of governmental, economic and societal functions, as well as public safety and the security of a nation. What distinguishes them from other types of infrastructure is their criticality and the far-reaching and detrimental impacts their potential disruption might generate. Generally, countries have defined critical infrastructure based on their national risk perception.[3] In India, the IT Act 2000 terms critical infrastructure as the "critical information infrastructure" and defines it as that "computer resource, the incapacitation or destruction of which, shall have a debilitating impact on national security, economy, public

DOI: 10.4324/9781003152910-3

Table 3.1 Critical sectors and types of threats

Critical sectors	Threats
• Telecommunication networks and other communication systems including internet; • Dams and water distribution systems; • Manufacturing plants; • Emergency and healthcare services; • Banking and digital financial services; • Stock market trading platforms; • Energy systems and power grids; • Nuclear reactors; • Defence industrial base and space systems; • Chemical industries; • Oil pipelines; • Transportation systems and signal management.	• Disruption or degradation of services; • Kinetic damage or destruction of critical infrastructure; • Loss of sensitive/strategic information due to data breaches; • Cascading effect-disruption in one sector can lead to disruptions in another.

Source: Gateway House Research

health or safety".[4] Likewise, in the United States, as per the President's Commission for Critical Infrastructure Protection, critical infrastructure includes, but is not limited to, telecommunications, energy, banking and finance, transportation, water systems and emergency services, both governmental and private.[5] Of course, this definition has evolved over the years.

In some countries, the focus has been on listing out critical sectors, rather than defining critical infrastructure, as per their priorities. However, some sectors stand out as common across many nations. These include transportation, energy, communication, financial and water systems.[6] As Table 3.1 explains, critical infrastructure spans many industries and sectors. As can be seen, many of these sectors are inter-related and inter-dependent, and they are supposed to provide round-the-clock functionality. Thus, any potential disruption or degradation of services can have an impact across sectors, particularly power, telecommunication and internet.

Much of the critical infrastructure is owned and run by the private sector, mainly the financial services and communications systems. As will be discussed later in the chapter, there are multiple challenges when it comes to protecting the private sector's critical infrastructure. One system which has not been listed in Table 3.1, but which has taken precedence in recent years, is the electoral infrastructure. Its security has emerged as a major concern, given that some nations have made targeted efforts to interfere with other nations' elections and the electoral process.

Stuxnet attack and its impact on India

Security researchers for years have discussed the ability of rogue actors to sabotage the operations of critical infrastructure,[7] but it was the Stuxnet virus of 2010 that demonstrated for the first time how such sabotage might pan out in real life. The virus was allegedly designed by the United States and Israel to target the Iranian nuclear programme.[8] Researchers at Symantec, an American cyber security firm, discovered the virus in July 2010, but they believed that it had existed for at least one year or more before their discovery.[9] The virus used two stolen digital certificates and multiple zero-day exploits to sabotage Siemens' Simatic S7 industrial control system, used for industrial automation and remote operations.[10] It was reportedly first used at Dimona, the headquarters of the Iranian nuclear programme.[11] Then, it eventually travelled to the Natanz uranium enrichment plant, where it spun the centrifuges out of control. This malfunction impacted the reactor operations and thus successfully slowed down the Iranian nuclear programme.[12]

The delivery of the virus to the Iranian reactors' computer systems suggested a highly sophisticated intelligence operation. These systems were "air-gapped" or "stand-alone", not connected to the internet. Yet the virus managed to infect them, which meant that it had been physically installed through Universal Serial Bus flash drives. This act suggested the role of an insider or a mole in the delivery of the virus.[13]

Cyber space doesn't recognise traditional sovereignty, and the Stuxnet virus was a clear example of this. It exploited the same vulnerabilities in computers from other countries as it did in Iran, and infected computer networks of several critical infrastructure facilities worldwide which ran on the Siemens systems. These included SCADA systems at manufacturing plants, power grids and oil pipelines. Reportedly, outside Iran, the virus infected over 100,000 systems in 115 countries.[14] Yet many organisations were reluctant to admit that the virus had hit their systems for fears of adverse impact on their economic fortunes and stock prices. The American energy company Chevron was one of the few which accepted that its network had been hit.[15] It can be safely argued that Stuxnet was an early but prime example of how businesses can get caught in nation-state-sponsored offensive cyber operations – sometimes as a target, but mostly as collateral damage or targets of opportunity. Pertinently, variations of Stuxnet, such as Duqu and Flame, soon followed and continued to disrupt computer networks worldwide.[16]

For India, this was also the first reported instance where the country was caught in the cross-fire of global geopolitical tensions. While the CERT-IN was quick to act, by issuing its first advisory in July 2010, by that time the virus had spread in the Indian systems.[17] As per media reports, it had infected between 10,000 to 80,000 computer systems.[18] These included the electricity grids in Gujarat and Haryana, as well as an Oil and Natural Gas Corporation offshore oil rig.[19] However, to date, it remains unclear whether the virus had infected computers in sensitive installations such as nuclear reactors. Beyond these infections, no significant disruption was reported at any Indian facilities. Nonetheless, these infections made India the third largest victim of the Stuxnet virus, after Iran and Indonesia.[20]

Vulnerability arising out of SCADA systems

Although Stuxnet infected several systems worldwide, its impact in terms of actual consequences was minor, as it only disrupted operations and didn't cause any kinetic damage. However, it demonstrated the extent of disruption that cyber attacks can have on the critical infrastructure and SCADA systems. These are computer-based industrial control systems. They monitor and control industrial processes and critical infrastructure equipment, and provide early warning of potential disaster situations. There is growing evidence – anecdotal and technical – that the SCADA systems constitute the weakest link in the protection of this critical infrastructure.

Many of these systems were installed 20–30 years ago, before internet connectivity and web-based applications became a norm. These systems' focus was on reliability than security; physical security was ensured, but information security was not a concern since these systems were "air-gapped", unconnected to a network.[21] They were therefore not built to deal with network-based threats or cyber attacks.[22] However, as remote operations and real-time information sharing became a norm, these systems were connected to a network, thereby closing the air-gap. This change made these systems vulnerable to attacks from not just the internet, but also business or enterprise network connections and other such networks.[23]

Network firewalls can prevent much malicious traffic, but with the wide availability of breaching techniques on the internet, hackers can bypass these security protocols.[24] The chief complication in case of a cyber attack on SCADA systems is that the systems cannot be de-activated/"taken off the network" for a forensic investigation of the attack. This is even more difficult when the SCADA or the industrial control systems deployed are performing a core function, such as power distribution or running a telecommunication network.

As per industry insiders, not only legacy systems, but also recently-installed SCADA systems in a networked environment are vulnerable to cyber attacks, since they have limited computational power to implement security protocols. According to a group of Australian security researchers, attacks on SCADA systems can be categorised as follows:

- IT services-based attack resulting from their manipulation or exploitation;
- Protocol-specific attack, which involves exploitation or misuse of automation protocol's rules to manipulate automation services or applications;
- Configuration-based attack, which consists of manipulation or exploitation of a critical system's endpoints; and
- Control process attack, which exploits or modifies process control logic or code executing an automation controller.[25]

Previously, their remote locations and the deployment of proprietary industrial networks had afforded SCADA systems "protection through isolation".[26] But that advantage no longer exists, as organisations adapt to the trend of standardisation of SCADA system hardware and software. Moreover, information on how to breach SCADA systems is freely available on the internet. These factors point to a vulnerability of SCADA systems to cyber attacks.

In December 2015, suspected Russian hackers breached into the SCADA systems of three Ukrainian power companies' networks – Prykarpattya Oblenergo,

Chernivtsi Oblenergo and Kiev Oblenergo – causing disruption of power supply in eight provinces.[27] As a result, more than 80,000 locals were left without power at the height of winter season. A DDoS attack on their call centres accompanied the breach in the power utilities' networks, which prevented people from reporting on the power outage.[28] This disruption was the first known instance of targeting a power utility through a cyber attack, where the motive was construed to be a geopolitical rivalry – in this case, between Russia and Ukraine over the disputed territory of Crimea.[29]

In India, the situation is no different vis-à-vis SCADA systems. Confidential data from CERT-IN reveals that hundreds of attacks on the SCADA systems of India occur annually, and anecdotal evidence suggests that their scale and frequency has increased over the years.[30] In September 2019, the nuclear reactor at Kudankulam in Tamil Nadu experienced a malware attack in which the reactor's administrative network was breached.[31] The malware was reportedly custom-built to breach the reactors' IT systems, signifying that it was a deliberate hack.[32] It was not clear who was behind the attack, but some reports speculated upon the role of North Korea.[33] Most recently, National Security Advisor Ajit Doval, in his address to a cyber security conference, noted that during the current outbreak of the COVID-19 pandemic, there had been a surge in attacks targeting the defence and critical infrastructure.[34]

Protecting election infrastructure

Another emerging security concern, not just for India but many other democracies, is the integrity of the electoral infrastructure. Given that elections are at the heart of any democracy, interfering in a democratic polity and manipulating elections has become a preferred strategy for many authoritarian regimes, as part of "hybrid warfare". The aim is to sow doubt in the minds of citizens about their democracies' credentials and legitimacy of their state institutions.

In 2016, malicious actors linked to the Russian government targeted the United States' election infrastructure during the presidential elections. As per the US Senate's Select Committee on Intelligence's inquiry, this targeting consisted of scanning of databases for vulnerabilities, attempted intrusions and, in some cases, successful penetration of a voter registration database.[35] Simultaneously, Russian intelligence-affiliated hackers targeted the presidential campaign of Hillary Clinton and the Democratic National Committee (the governing body of the Democratic party).[36] Since then, similar cyber attacks have been reported from Australia,[37] Indonesia,[38] Canada,[39] Brazil,[40] the United Kingdom[41] and many other democracies. These attacks have targeted computer networks of the national parliament, political parties and voter databases. Interestingly, some of these attacks were accompanied by instances of cyber-enabled foreign interference such as disinformation campaigns on social media platforms and "fake news", funded and directed from abroad.[42] In the case of the United States, for instance, a data analytics firm, Cambridge Analytica, was accused of running a campaign targeted at American voters on Facebook.[43] Multiple reports highlighted the firm's linkages with the Russian government.⁴⁴ The firm had reportedly harvested data on 50 million Facebook users in an illegal manner.⁴⁵

These attacks have prompted national election authorities to step up their cyber security preparedness and secure their election systems from sabotage. For instance, in the United States, the Department of Homeland Security has now designated federal elections as part of the critical infrastructure.⁴⁶ Likewise, the Canadian government's cyber security agencies have worked with citizens and national political parties to protect elections from cyber attacks and foreign interference.⁴⁷

India has not seen such cyber attacks – not yet, but it has been at the receiving end of many foreign disinformation campaigns, and not just during elections. To ensure the inviolability of the election infrastructure, the Election Commission, which is tasked with maintaining the sanctity of India's electoral process, has taken several steps.⁴⁸ Apart from putting in place stringent measures to make the Electronic Voting Machines tamper and hack-proof, the commission has made mandatory use of Voter Verifiable Paper Audit Trail (machines which confirm voting to the voters) for auditing the process.⁴⁹ In addition, the commission created the post of Chief Information Security Officer in 2017 to supervise cyber security measures for the organisation and ensure compliance with them.⁵⁰ To be clear, India has not yet categorised election infrastructure as critical infrastructure. These steps aside, authorities have found it challenging to grapple with disinformation campaigns and "fake news", but even the technology majors and social media platforms have struggled in countering this phenomenon, given the sheer speed with which such content is created and spreads.

Mitigating critical infrastructure vulnerabilities

Defending against the threat of cyber attacks on critical infrastructure requires a systemic approach, with collaboration amongst stakeholders spread across public and private sectors, as well as across the jurisdictions. After experiencing the infections caused by the Stuxnet virus, the Indian government set up the NCIIPC in 2014.⁵¹ This centre, set up under the aegis of the technical intelligence agency, the NTRO, works with the public and private sectors to plug gaps in their critical infrastructure systems. The main contribution of the centre has been to bring out detailed guidelines to secure critical infrastructure.⁵² These provide a comprehensive overview of the critical infrastructure protection plan in India. The guidelines are divided into five families of controls: planning controls, implementation controls, operational controls, disaster recovery/business continuity planning controls and reporting and accountability controls.⁵³ Also, the centre regularly brings out the Common Vulnerabilities and Exposures reports.⁵⁴ These provide a comprehensive overview to critical infrastructure operators of the vulnerabilities discovered in cyber space.

Before the NCIIPC, in 2012, the NSCS had worked with the private sector through a joint working group to identify gaps in India's cyber security.⁵⁵ Its report had identified critical infrastructure organisations as being at higher risk, and had therefore recommended defining enhanced standards and guidelines.

Apart from the NCIIPC, there are also sectoral CERTs, including CERT-Thermal, CERT-Hydro, CERT-Transmission and CERT-Distribution. The first three CERTs are also part of the Information Sharing and Analysis Centre, which disseminates information about cyber incidents in the power sector.[56] Another government agency which works on SCADA security is Pune-based C-DAC, which functions under the MEITY. The agency provides a security testbed system for assessing the vulnerabilities in SCADA and other industrial control systems.[57]

While the government has sought to collaborate with the private sector in mitigating the vulnerabilities in critical infrastructure protection, in practice, such collaboration has proved difficult to achieve. This is ironic, since businesses have shown enthusiasm in working with the government on other aspects of cyber security, like training of IT personnel and combating cyber crimes. Multiple issues, including trust deficit, competitive business environment and absence of adequate capacity (technical and forensic) have hindered cooperation between the state and the private sector on the plugging of SCADA vulnerabilities.

One of the significant challenges has been the reluctance among the private sector to disclose the vulnerability of their SCADA systems. Whenever they are faced with a cyber attack or a data breach on their critical infrastructure systems, businesses have resorted to plugging the security gaps in their systems. However, they hesitate to talk about it for fear of exposing themselves and losing a competitive edge over rivals. Moreover, Indian regulators have often complained that the businesses' focus on plugging the SCADA vulnerabilities is a tactical, short-term business-specific response, which overlooks the possibility of concerted cyber warfare by hostile nations against India. This constricted approach works against ensuring comprehensive SCADA security.

Given the mutual distrust and vulnerability of both public and private players, the solution will involve jointly addressing the problem in the form of a public-private-partnership. This should focus on building an institutional framework, expanding and deepening capacity and creating security standards and strict audits. The NCIIPC has, to some extent, bridged this trust deficit by following the dictum that cyber security is a shared responsibility.[58]

Within businesses, another major challenge is the lack of awareness on cyber security of the critical infrastructure. The absence of adequate understanding and cyber security expertise at the senior management or Board of Directors level is a perennial challenge. The shortage of trained members of the workforce accentuates this challenge. Multiple market research studies have pointed out the woeful shortage of cyber security expertise in India and, according to industry insiders, this is even more so for SCADA security expertise.[59,60]

Conclusion

There is little doubt that securing critical infrastructure is the most dominant concern for India's cyber security. The country may not have witnessed the sort of cyber attack on critical infrastructure as depicted in the film Die Hard 4.0,[61] but vulnerabilities of SCADA systems are continually expanding, and with the advent of the Internet of Things-based devices and networks, they are further set to expand. Therefore, only an integrated approach involving collaboration between the government and the private sector will yield the desired security of the critical infrastructure. Such an approach will also push India's digital economy ambitions.

Notes

1 "India's Trillion-Dollar Digital Opportunity," Ministry of Electronics and Information Technology, accessed March 21, 2020, www.meity.gov.in/writereaddata/files/india_trillion-dollar_digital_opportunity.pdf.
2 Shane Harris, *@War: The Rise of the Military-Internet Complex* (New York: Houghton Mifflin Harcourt, 2014), 46.
3 A useful resource on definitions of critical infrastructure is Tim Maurer and Robert Morgus, "Compilation of Existing Cybersecurity and Information Security Related Definitions," New America Report, 2014: 44–50.
4 "The Information Technology Act, 2000," National Informatics Centre, accessed May 11, 2020, www.indiacode.nic.in/bitstream/123456789/1999/3/A2000-21.pdf.
5 "The Clinton Administration's Policy on Critical Infrastructure Protection: Presidential Decision Directive 63," The White House, accessed May 11, 2020, https://clinton whitehouse4.archives.gov/WH/EOP/NSC/html/documents/NSCDoc3.html.
6 C. Gallais and E. Filiol, "Critical Infrastructure: Where Do We Stand Today? A Comprehensive and Comparative Study of the Definitions of a Critical Infrastructure," *Journal of Information Warfare* 16, no. 1 (2017): 70.
7 Emily Frye, "The Tragedy of the Cybercommons: Overcoming Fundamental Vulnerabilities to Critical Infrastructures in a Networked World," *The Business Lawyer* 58, no. 1 (November 2002): 349–382.
8 David Kushner, "The Real Story of Stuxnet," *IEEE Spectrum*, February 26, 2013, https://spectrum.ieee.org/telecom/security/the-real-story-of-stuxnet.
9 "W32.Stuxnet Dossier Version 1.3," Wired, accessed August 15, 2020, www.wired.com/images_blogs/threatlevel/2010/11/w32_stuxnet_dossier.pdf.
10 Thomas M. Chen, *Cyberterrorism after Stuxnet* (Carlisle, PA: Strategic Studies Institute, US Army War College, 2014).
11 William J. Broad, John Markoff and David E. Sanger, "Israeli Test on Worm Called Crucial in Iran Nuclear Delay," *The New York Times*, January 15, 2011, www.nytimes.com/2011/01/16/world/middleeast/16stuxnet.html.
12 Ellen Nakashima and Joby Warrick, "Stuxnet Was Work of U.S. and Israeli Experts, Officials Say," *The Washington Post*, June 2, 2012, www.washingtonpost.com/world/national-security/stuxnet-was-work-of-us-and-israeli-experts-officials-say/2012/06/01/gJQAInEy6U_story.html.
13 William Gross, "Insider Threat," in *Computer and Information Security Handbook (Third Edition)*, ed. John R. Vacca (Cambridge: Elsevier-Morgan Kaufmann Publishers, 2017), 531.
14 See n. 8.
15 Rachael King, "Stuxnet Infected Chevron's IT Network," *The Wall Street Journal*, November 8, 2012, https://blogs.wsj.com/cio/2012/11/08/stuxnet-infected-chevrons-it-network/.
16 "Gauss: Abnormal Distribution," Kaspersky Lab, accessed August 15, 2020, https://media.kasperskycontenthub.com/wp-content/uploads/sites/43/2018/03/20134940/kaspersky-lab-gauss.pdf.

17 "CERT-In Advisory CIAD-2010–0051," CERT-India, accessed August 18, 2020, www.cert-in.org.in/s2cMainServlet?pageid=PUBVLNOTES02&VLCODE=CIAD-2009-0051.
18 Javed Anwar, "Cyber War on between US and Iran; India Caught in Crossfire," *The Economic Times*, August 20, 2012, https://economictimes.indiatimes.com/tech/internet/cyber-war-on-between-us-and-iran-india-caught-in-crossfire/articleshow/15567740.cms.
19 Pierre Fitter, "Stuxnet Attack Wakes India Up to Threat to Critical Infrastructure," *India Today*, September 5, 2012, http://indiatoday.intoday.in/story/stuxnet-cyber-war-critical-infrastructure-of-india-ntro/1/216107.html.
20 See n. 8.
21 Eric D. Knapp and Joel Thomas Langill, *Industrial Network Security: Securing Critical Infrastructure Networks for Smart Grid, SCADA, and Other Industrial Control Systems* (Waltham, MA: Syngress, 2015), 42.
22 Sameer Patil, "India's Vulnerable SCADA Systems," *Gateway House*, June 17, 2014, www.gatewayhouse.in/indias-vulnerable-scada-systems/.
23 B. Zhu, A. Joseph and S. Sastry, "A Taxonomy of Cyber Attacks on SCADA Systems," 2011 International Conference on Internet of Things and 4th International Conference on Cyber, Physical and Social Computing, Dalian, 2011, 380–388.
24 Pedro Taveras N., "SCADA Live Forensics: Real Time Data Acquisition Process to Detect, Prevent or Evaluate Critical Situations," 1st Annual International Interdisciplinary Conference, 2013, 253–262.
25 Nicholas Rodofile, Kenneth Radke and Ernest Foo, "Extending the Cyber-Attack Landscape for SCADA-Based Critical Infrastructure. International Journal of Critical Infrastructure Protection," *International Journal of Critical Infrastructure Protection* 25 (June 2019): 14–35.
26 See n. 23.
27 "Cyber Attacks on the Ukrainian Grid: What You Should Know," FireEye, accessed August 15, 2020, www.fireeye.com/content/dam/fireeye-www/global/en/solutions/pdfs/fe-cyber-attacks-ukrainian-grid.pdf.
28 BBC News, "Hackers Behind Ukraine Power Cuts, Says US Report," February 26, 2016, www.bbc.com/news/technology-35667989.
29 Sameer Patil, "Geopolitical Rivalries in Cyberspace," *Gateway House*, February 18, 2016, www.gatewayhouse.in/geopolitics-and-cyber-attack-in-ukraine/.
30 See n. 21.
31 "Press Release," Nuclear Power Corporation of India Limited, accessed August 15, 2020, https://npcil.nic.in/writereaddata/Orders/20191030123734696017lNews_3010 2019_01.pdf.
32 Saikat Datta and Anand Venkatanarayanan, "Cyberattack Scare Dogs India's Nuclear Plants," *Asia Times*, October 20, 2019, https://asiatimes.com/2019/10/cyberattack-scare-dogs-indias-nuclear-plants/.
33 Debak Das, "An Indian Nuclear Power Plant Suffered a Cyberattack: Here's What You Need to Know," *The Washington Post*, November 4, 2019, www.washingtonpost.com/politics/2019/11/04/an-indian-nuclear-power-plant-suffered-cyberattack-heres-what-you-need-know/.
34 Kerala Police (@KeralaPoliceOfficial), "c0c0n 2020: Keynote Speech by Shri Ajit Doval, National Security Advisor," YouTube Video, September 17, 2020, www.youtube.com/watch?v=m2ctyqdgIzg.
35 "Russian Targeting of Election Infrastructure during the 2016 Election: Summary of Initial Findings and Recommendations," U.S. Senate Select Committee on Intelligence, accessed June 15, 2020, www.intelligence.senate.gov/publications/russia-inquiry.
36 "Report on the Investigation into Russian Interference in the 2016 Presidential Election," Department of Justice, accessed June 15, 2020, www.justice.gov/storage/report.pdf.
37 Bill Shorten, "Parliament Cyber Attack Hits Major Parties," *SBS News*, February 18, 2019, www.sbs.com.au/news/parliament-cyber-attack-hits-major-parties.

38 The Straits Times, "Indonesian Polls under Attack by Foreign Hackers: Official," March 14, 2019, www.straitstimes.com/asia/se-asia/indonesian-polls-under-attack-by-foreign-hackers-official.
39 Janice Dickson, "Foreign Interference 'Very Likely' in Canada's 2019 Election, Federal Security Agency Warns," *The Globe and Mail*, April 8, 2019, www.theglobeandmail.com/politics/article-foreign-interference-likely-in-canadas-2019-election-federal/.
40 Bruno Benevides, "Russian Hackers Are Trying To Interfere in Brazilian Elections, Cybersecurity Firm Says," *Folha De S. Paulo*, October 5, 2018, https://www1.folha.uol.com.br/internacional/en/world/2018/10/russian-hackers-are-trying-to-interfere-in-brazilian-elections-cybersecurity-firm-says.shtml.
41 "Statement: Cyber Incidents Affecting Political Parties," UK National Cyber Security Centre, November 12, 2019, www.ncsc.gov.uk/news/cyber-incidents-affecting-political-parties.
42 Sarah O'Connor, Fergus Hanson, Emilia Currey and Tracy Beattie, "Cyber-Enabled Foreign Interference in Elections and Referendums," *ASPI International Cyber Policy Centre*, Policy Brief Report No. 41/2020, www.aspi.org.au/report/cyber-enabled-foreign-interference-elections-and-referendums.
43 Mark Zuckerberg (@zuck), "Update on the Cambridge Analytica Situation," Facebook, March 22, 2018, www.facebook.com/zuck/posts/10104712037900071?pnref=story.
44 James Lamond and Jeremy Venook, "Blunting Foreign Interference Efforts by Learning the Lessons of the Past," *Centre for American Progress*, September 2, 2020, www.americanprogress.org/issues/security/reports/2020/09/02/489865/blunting-foreign-interference-efforts-learning-lessons-past/.
45 Matthew Rosenberg, Nicholas Confessore and Carole Cadwalladr, "How Trump Consultants Exploited the Facebook Data of Millions," *The New York Times*, March 17, 2018, www.nytimes.com/2018/03/17/us/politics/cambridge-analytica-trump-campaign.html.
46 "Election Infrastructure Security," U.S. Cybersecurity & Infrastructure Security Agency, www.cisa.gov/election-security.
47 "Protecting Democracy," Government of Canada, March 19, 2020, www.canada.ca/en/democratic-institutions/services/protecting-democracy.html.
48 Sameer Patil, "The Cyber Security Imperative for India's Elections," *Gateway House*, April 18, 2019, www.gatewayhouse.in/cyber-security-india-election/.
49 "Cyber Security Newsletter May, 2018," *Election Commission of India*, May 2018, https://eci.gov.in/files/file/5685-cyber-security-newsletter-may2018/.
50 Ibid.
51 "Information Technology (National Critical Information Infrastructure Protection Centre and Manner of Performing Functions and Duties) Rules, 2013," Ministry of Electronics and Information Technology, January 16, 2014, http://meity.gov.in/sites/upload_files/dit/files/GSR_19(E).pdf.
52 "Guidelines for Protection of Critical Information Infrastructure Version 2.0," National Critical Information Infrastructure Protection Centre, January 16, 2015, https://nciipc.gov.in/documents/NCIIPC_Guidelines_V2.pdf.
53 Ibid., 11
54 "Common Vulnerabilities and Exposures (CVE) Report," National Critical Information Infrastructure Protection Centre 7, no. 18, September 16–30, 2020, https://nciipc.gov.in/documents/16_30_Sep20_CVE.pdf.
55 "Recommendations of Joint Working Group on Engagement with Private Sector on Cyber Security," Confederation of Indian Industries, https://cii.in/WebCMS/Upload/JWG%20report.pdf.
56 "ISAC-Power," Indian Computer Emergency Response Team, www.cert-in.org.in/s2c MainServlet?pageid=ISACPower.
57 "Industrial Control System Security Test Bed (ICSSTB)," C-DAC, www.cdac.in/index.aspx?id=pe_ngcs_CIG_ICSSTB.

58 Saikat Datta, "The NCIIPC and Its Evolving Framework," *Observer Research Foundation*, November 3, 2016, www.orfonline.org/expert-speak/nciipc-its-evolving-framework/.
59 "Cyber Security India Market," PWC-DSCI, accessed June 15, 2020, www.pwc.in/assets/pdfs/consulting/cyber-security/cyber-security-india-market.pdf.
60 "About Industry," DSCI, accessed June 15, 2020, www.dsci.in/industry-development/.
61 David Braue, "Be Afraid: Die Hard 4 Reveals a Real Threat," *The Sydney Morning Herald*, May 28, 2012, www.smh.com.au/technology/be-afraid–die-hard-4-reveals-a-real-threat-20120528–1zeg0.html.

4 Building resilient digital payment systems[1]

Introduction

In the last few years, India has made substantial efforts to embrace digital or cashless payment systems by reducing reliance on cash transactions. The adoption of digital payment systems is part of India's ambitious effort to transition to digital governance, where IT is being harnessed for delivering citizen-centric government services. This digitisation is taking place within a short period, and promises to overhaul the outlook and delivery of basic government services spanning banking and other financial payment services, healthcare, education, subsidies, taxation, among others.

Initiatives like IndiaStack have allowed the government to utilise IT in an affordable and scalable manner to try and achieve financial inclusion and expand the use of digital payment systems.[2] The introduction of new products through the use of financial technological (fintech) innovations, such as Prepaid Payment Instruments (PPI), commonly known as "mobile wallets", supplements this. This shift towards digital economy promises higher tax revenue, expansion of e-commerce and an opportunity to tackle terrorist financing and money laundering. This transition to the digital economy is also an opportunity to create a digital ecosystem of banking, financial, e-commerce and associated apps and services.

India's sustained push in the digital payment space is centred on the JAM trinity (the Pradhan Mantri Jan-Dhan Yojana initiative to make basic financial services available to all, linkage of Aadhaar national identity cards to government subsidy payments and promotion of mobile payment systems). This is an ambitious endeavour, which certainly can be replicated and adapted globally – not just in emerging economies, but also in developed economies which are struggling with legacy financial systems and have hit a plateau in financial inclusion. However, this shift towards digital payments is taking place when cyber threats to payment systems are expanding. Although India has taken extensive cyber security measures, its digital payment infrastructure continues to lack resilience. In this context, this chapter analyses the cyber security of India's digital retail payments industry, efforts to safeguard it and the challenges involved.

Digital payments ecosystem

In the last ten years, India's regulators and payment industry participants have taken multiple initiatives in the digital payments space (Table 4.1). A significant

DOI: 10.4324/9781003152910-4

milestone in this was setting up of the National Payments Corporation of India (NPCI) by 56 major state-owned and private-sector banks in 2008 to manage retail payment systems.[3] In 2012, NPCI launched RuPay – an Indian brand for retail electronic payments.[4] The NPCI then innovated the Unified Payments Interface (UPI), a fund transfer mechanism.[5] Its uniqueness was that it allowed instantaneous fund transfers between two bank accounts by using mobile numbers associated with the account, Quick Response codes, Aadhar numbers or virtual payment addresses, which were linked to bank accounts. A key enabler for UPI was seeding of personal and biometric Aadhaar data with individual bank account information. These transactions, executed through the authentication of Aadhaar data, gave rise to the Aadhaar-enabled Payment Systems (AEPS).[6] Besides UPI and AEPS, another critical element of the NPCI network is the National Financial Switch (NFS), a shared Automated Teller Machine (ATM) network. The NFS, which currently has 1,176 members, interconnects its members and more than 2.50 lakh ATM switches.[7]

Digital payment systems came into sharp focus following the Indian government's move to withdraw the high-value currency notes of Rs. 500 and 1000 in November 2016. Data from the RBI suggested that the volume and value of digital payment transactions post-November 2016 had dramatically increased, particularly for the mobile wallets and Point of Sale (PoS) terminals.[8]

At present, India's digital retail payment systems can be divided as follows, in AEPS (which uses Aadhar data for authentication) and non-AEPS:

Table 4.1 India's digital payment nodes

AEPS	
UPI-based applications	Mobile applications for payment and related transactions
Micro-ATM	Modified PoS terminals used by the business correspondents of any bank to make transactions
*99# service	Mobile banking service based on the Unstructured Supplementary Service Data (USSD) communication protocol – a communications technology used by mobile phones for payment transactions
BHIM Aadhaar Pay	UPI-based mobile application for merchants to receive payments from customers over the counter through Aadhaar authentication
Non-AEPS payment systems	
Prepaid Payment Instruments	Digital applications that store consumer payment information and carry out payment transactions. Commonly known as "mobile wallets" such as PayTM, MobiKwik and Oxigen
PoS terminal	Payments made at retail establishments using debit or credit cards on physical equipment
Online banking	Mobile or internet-based banking applications for payment transactions and other banking services
Neobanks	Virtual banking services offered through a mobile application utilising fintech

Source: Gateway House Research[9]

These payment systems are also a work in progress, as the Indian financial sector is deploying new products, payment formats and technologies such as mobile wallets and Near-field communication technology. One notable aspect here is the absence of crypto-currencies such as Bitcoin. The RBI has barred Indian citizens from trading in or using these currencies. In 2018, it also prohibited banks from providing financial services to crypto-currency exchanges. However, in March 2020, the Supreme Court of India ruled that while the RBI had the power to regulate these currencies, RBI's 2018 prohibition was disproportionate and therefore unconstitutional.[10]

Growing cyber risks to payment systems worldwide

India's adoption of digital payments comes at a time when the banking and financial services sector is becoming a sustained target of hacking and data breaches. As noted in earlier chapters, since the 2007 disruptions in Estonia, cyber attacks have become increasingly precise, revealing the exponential growth in the sophistication of the cyber criminals to commit fraud – not just by technological advances, but also by innovative ways to commit crimes. As the example of the US NSA shows, states have developed sophisticated capabilities to exploit vulnerabilities in other countries' computer networks – much like actual weapons.

In many cases, foreign governments have used proxy non-state actors – hacktivists, hacking groups and organised cyber criminals – for launching offensive cyber operations and netting the cyber crime proceeds. Such attacks have blurred the state/non-state actor distinction. This was evident in the case of the North Korea-backed APT38 cyber operation of 2018, which repeatedly targeted financial institutions' SWIFT (also known as Society for Worldwide Interbank Financial Telecommunication) payment transactions and attempted to steal over USD $1.1 billion.[11]

These non-state actors have also brought more resources and ingenuity. The targeting of more than 100 banks and other financial institutions in 40 countries (mostly in Europe) by Carbanak, a criminal syndicate led by a Spain-based mastermind, demonstrates this growing threat. Between 2013 and 2018, through a malware attack on banks, this syndicate stole more than €1 billion.[12]

While rogue actors have honed their capacity to launch severe cyber attacks and cause intense damage, tackling them has become challenging due to the problem of attribution – difficulties in attributing them to a particular region or specific state actor. Moreover, these criminal acts span multiple jurisdictions – their consequences are no longer restricted to the location where the crime took place. The issue of jurisdiction is incredibly daunting since, for well-known cases of cyber crime, nations seamlessly exchange information. Still, for the daily occurrences of cyber crime, they have found it challenging to replicate the same kind of cooperation.

Trends in cyber attacks on India's payments system

As seen in Chapter 2, a review of cyber attacks on India's computer networks, whether government or commercial, reveals that India has not witnessed a large-scale disruptive attack, as has been the case in some other countries. However, there have been numerous persistent unauthorised access incidents and data breaches targeting the financial sector. This is also a reflection of the global trend where banks have remained a sustained target for advanced cyber crimes, with a massive sophistication of the malware leading to unauthorised access, data theft and disruption of services.

The most severe cyber incident involving the Indian financial sector remains that of the malware attack on the Hitachi Payment Services (a payment subsidiary of Hitachi Ltd. Japan) in 2016.[13] In this incident, a sophisticated malware was injected into India-based servers of Hitachi Payment Services. This attack enabled unauthorised access to the debit card data. The intrusion remained undetected for a long time, and resulted in an economic loss totalling Rs. 1.3 crore. It also forced 19 major Indian public and private sector banks to replace 3.2 million ATM-cum-debit cards.[14]

However, it is not just the centralised databases of the retail payment systems that are being targeted. Hacking groups and cyber crime syndicates are also carrying out "social engineering" attacks by going after individual users and banking staff to gain unauthorised access to computer networks.[15] The most preferred medium for this is phishing emails, which entice the users to click on a link that installs malware or ransomware on their systems, enabling them to harvest personal data or steal login credentials. In 2016, hackers used this tactic to lure an employee of one of the country's largest public-sector banks, the Union Bank of India. They subsequently installed malware in the bank's servers and gained access to its payment systems. This allowed hackers to siphon USD $170 million from its foreign-exchange accounts. Fortunately, with timely intervention, the bank fully recovered the stolen money.

However, this is not always the case. In many other instances, money is either only partially recovered or lost altogether. In February 2018, City Union Bank, a Tamil Nadu-based bank, suffered a hacking incident in which it lost nearly USD $2 million in three remittance transactions.[16] The bank was successfully able to block two transactions to the tune of USD $872,000.[17] Maharashtra-based Cosmos Bank was not so fortunate. The bank became a victim of the malware attack, carried out by the North Korea-linked Lazarus hacker group, in August 2018. Consequently, the bank lost Rs. 94.42 crore through ATMs and online transfers, which it never recovered.[18,19] These have been some of the noteworthy instances of financial losses arising out of cyber attacks on digital payment systems. However, many such instances never come to light, as reporting on cyber security incidents and data breaches is still not mandatory.

A debilitating cyber attack on financial infrastructure, such as banks and payment systems, can lead to economic loss or disruption of service, and potentially even set off a recession, if not mitigated in time. But beyond economic costs, there are also other costs, as seen in cases of cyber attacks worldwide. These include loss of proprietary financial data and reputational costs, and hence future business opportunities and degrading of economic prospects. A case in point is the 2017 data breach involving Equifax, a US-based consumer credit reporting agency, which lost more than USD $3 billion in stock market value after it reported a data breach.[20] Then there are the liability issues. For instance, Anthem, an American insurance company, was forced to pay USD $115 million to settle consumer claims over a 2015 data breach that exposed records of approximately 78.8 million consumers.[21] While cyber attacks on the Indian financial sector have so far not seen these developments, as more digitisation of the economy takes place, banks and other financial institutions will have to pay attention to these risks and mitigate them.

So far, what has been observed is that companies are still playing catch-up with these growing threats. Companies are prioritising cyber security, but many times cyber security compliance is treated as a mere formality, as comprehensive threat management is overlooked. Inadequate budgets and insufficient cyber security expertise at the senior management – what is termed as the C-level/C-suite – add to these challenges. There is also over-reliance on cyber insurance, as some businesses believe that a grave cyber incident that could imperil their business is unlikely. But as the next section illustrates, threat vectors exist at every level of the digital payment system, which necessitates the required investment in cyber security.

Mapping potential threat vectors

Given the innovations in digital technology, cyber threats are continually evolving, which make India's digital payment systems susceptible to several threat vectors. The table below maps and explains node-specific vulnerabilities, channels and perpetrators for the payment system (Table 4.2).

Automation and computerisation of banking systems in India primarily happened in the last 15 years. As a result, most Indian banks have been able to use modern IT infrastructure to start automation of their core banking processes, so they have been able to avoid cyber security issues associated with the legacy systems. However, advanced malware now poses the most significant cyber security threat to the banking and payment systems. As seen in the case of the 2016 Union Bank of India hack, specific malware targeting banking systems is now a reality. This malware threat is being accentuated due to weak cyber hygiene practices.

Documented poor cyber hygiene practices specific to India include use of pirated and outdated software including operating systems, connecting standalone devices to the internet, using same machines for personal and work purposes, sharing passwords and responding to phishing emails and vishing. Additionally, internet use in India is driven by low-end smart phones, with even lower security standards. This has made cyber hygiene the weakest link for the security of digital payment systems. A trend pointed out by Indian payment industry professionals is the growing frequency of mobile malware, which seeks to capitalise on this lack of cyber hygiene.[22] The government has taken multiple steps on cyber hygiene education, including the Pradhan Mantri Gramin Digital Saksharta Abhiyan,[23] which is specifically aimed at countering phishing emails and vishing, but these will need to be expanded to instil a culture of cyber hygiene and safety.

As India's dependence on digital payment systems deepens, mainly through the UPI, AEPS mobile wallets and neo-banks, the vulnerabilities cited here are expanding the threat landscape. To address these, the government has taken multiple steps, and the next section discusses this.

Table 4.2 Vulnerabilities, channels and perpetrators

Where (Node)	Why (Vulnerability)	How (Channel)	Who (Perpetrator)	What (Implication)
Aadhaar-Enabled Payment System (BHIM app, BHIM Aadhaar pay)				
UPI applications	– Biometric data – Centralised data storage – Lack of patched system (computer with outdated software)	– DDoS attack – Malware injection	– Adversarial states – Organised criminal syndicates – Hackers' collective – Individual hackers	– Identity theft – Doxing (leaking of personal sensitive and financial data for coercion)
Customer's bank	– Lack of environment patch update hygiene – Insider threat	– Malware injection – APT – Internal network sniffer – Man in the middle attack	– Terrorist groups – Hacktivists – Rogue employees	– Data breach – Fraud and economic loss – Data breach
Receiving bank	– Lack of environment patch update hygiene – Insider threat	– Malware injection – APT – Internal network sniffer		– Data breach – Fraud and economic loss – Loss of proprietary financial data – Cyber-enabled espionage – Loss of reputation
*99# (USSD) service				
USSD gateway (GSM mobile *99#)	– Deficient cyber hygiene – Lack of or insufficient encryption	– Social engineering attack – Man in the middle attack	– Adversarial states – Organised criminal syndicates – Hackers' collective – Individual hackers	– Data breach and loss – Identity theft – Doxing
Customer's bank	– Lack of patched system – Insider threat	– Social engineering attack – Malware injection – APT – Internal network sniffer – Man in the middle attack	– Terrorist groups – Hacktivists – Rogue employees	– Data breach – Fraud and economic loss – Data breach
Receiving bank	– Lack of environment patch update hygiene – Insider threat	– Malware injection – APT – Internal network sniffer		– Data breach – Fraud and economic loss – Loss of proprietary financial data

Building resilient digital payment systems

PPI/Mobile wallets

Component	Vulnerabilities	Threats	Threat actors	Impact
Customer's mobile wallet	– Lack of Two-Factor Authentication	– SIM card swapping and cloning – DDoS attack – Fake wallet apps	– Adversarial states – Organised criminal syndicates – Hackers' collective – Individual hackers – Terrorist groups – Hacktivists – Rogue employees	– Identity theft – Disruption of service – Doxing – Economic loss – Data breach
Payment gateway or switch	– Lack of or insufficient encryption	– Man in the middle attack – DDoS attack		– Data breach
Payment processor	– Lack of or insufficient encryption	– Man in the middle attack – DDoS attack		
Customer's bank	– Lack of patched system – Insider threat	– Malware injection – APT – Internal network sniffer – Man in the middle attack		– Data breach – Fraud and economic loss
Issuing bank	– Lack of environment patch update hygiene – Insider threat	– Malware injection – APT – Internal network sniffer		– Data breach – Data breach – Fraud and economic loss

PoS Terminal and Micro-ATM

Component	Vulnerabilities	Threats	Threat actors	Impact
PoS terminal	– Deficient cyber hygiene	– Card cloning – Digital black markets – Social engineering attack	– Adversarial states – Organised criminal syndicates – Hackers' collective – Individual hackers – Terrorist groups – Hacktivists – Rogue employees	– Financial data loss – Identity theft – Doxing – Data breach – Data breach
Payment processor	– Lack of or insufficient encryption	– Man in the middle attack		
Acquiring bank	– Lack of environment patch update hygiene – Insider threat	– Malware injection – APT – Internal network sniffer – Man in the middle attack		– Data breach – Fraud and economic loss
Payment brand's network	– Lack of or insufficient encryption			– Data breach
Issuing bank	– Lack of environment patch update hygiene – Insider threat	– Malware injection – APT – Internal network sniffer		– Data breach – Fraud and economic loss

(Continued)

Table 4.2 (Continued)

Where (Node)	Why (Vulnerability)	How (Channel)	Who (Perpetrator)	What (Implication)
		Online banking		
Customer's bank website	– Deficient cyber hygiene – Rooted devices or apps	– DDoS Attack – SIM card swapping – Social engineering attack	– Adversarial states – Organised criminal syndicates – Hackers' collective – Individual hackers – Terrorist groups – Hacktivists – Rogue employees	– Financial data loss – Identity theft – Disruption of service – Doxing – Data breach – Fraud and economic loss – Data breach – Data breach – Fraud and economic loss – Loss of reputation
Customer's bank	– Lack of environment patch update hygiene – Insider threat	– Malware injection – APT – Internal network sniffer		
Receiving bank	– Lack of environment patch update hygiene – Insider threat	– Malware injection – APT – Internal network sniffer		
Vulnerabilities				
Biometric data	Compromise of the biometric data such as fingerprints and iris can potentially result in spoofing of identity.			
Centralised data storage	Centralised storage of data is often described as a "honey pot", which entices users to hack into the databases.			
Lack of patched system	Outdated and vulnerable systems, if not patched adequately in time, can be sitting ducks for cyber-attacks.			
Insider threat	Former and/or current employees who have access to critical information, including financial and customer data, can expose banks to cyber-attacks.			
Lack of or insufficient encryption	Lack of or insufficient encryption of transiting data, using protocols such as SSL or TSL, can expose it to interception.			
Lack of cyber hygiene	Many Indian internet users, being first-generation users, lack knowledge of safe practices – dos and don'ts – to protect themselves.			
Two-Factor Authentication	If the customer's mobile phone is not secure enough, two-factor authentication can be used to permit fraudulent transactions.			
Unsecured mobile phones	Internet use in India is driven by low-end mobile phones, which come with even lower security standards, making them vulnerable to hacking.			

Channels

DDoS attack	An attack technique in which multiple computer systems are used to target a single system such as a payment server, internet banking website or mobile application, by overloading it with superfluous traffic and rendering it inoperative.
Malware injection	Malware dispatched by hackers to infect individual systems or a large network, by targeting existing software vulnerabilities, especially on unpatched systems.
APT	Sophisticated hacking technique used to penetrate a network and remain undetected for an extended time, harvesting sensitive personal and financial information.
Internal network sniffer	Technique used to capture data when it is being transmitted over a network, especially unencrypted data like usernames and passwords.
Man in the middle attack	Attack technique where saboteurs steal data during transit to carry out fraudulent payment transactions.
Social engineering attack	Attack technique that lures individuals to divulge confidential information or perform actions to gain privileged access to restricted systems.
SIM card swapping	Tactic where a hacker tricks a mobile carrier to switch a user's phone number to a SIM card owned by the hackers; this is then used to steal sensitive personal and financial information, and also for two-factor authentication.
Fake wallet apps	Mobile wallet apps which replicate the original genuine apps to prompt users to divulge wallet passwords, private keys and other sensitive personal financial information.
Carding	Frauds committed with stolen but active credit cards.
Digital black markets	Digital black markets offer easy access to computer hacking tools, software vulnerability data, social engineering attack tools and malicious software.

Source: Gateway House Research[24]

Regulatory framework to protect payments system

The IT Act 2000 (amended in 2008) and the NCSP 2013 act as the umbrella frameworks to tackle the expanding cyber threats to digital payments. These have been accompanied by multiple issue-specific guidelines, advisories, technical frameworks and standards (Table 4.3).

The RBI, as the principal regulator, has issued cyber security frameworks covering various financial institutions. In 2016, it brought a Cyber Security Framework for banks, which mandated the latter to set up a Security Operations Centre (SOC) to detect cyber security incidents.[25] The banks were asked to report these incidents to the Indian Banks – Center for Analysis of Risks and Threats (IB-CART). In addition, it instructed banks to adopt and implement cyber security policies with emphasis on organisational resilience and cyber hygiene. Despite RBI's instructions, many smaller banks are still yet to establish a SOC. RBI has issued similar frameworks for the urban cooperative banks as well as PPI (mobile wallet) operators.[26,27] Specifically, the PPI operators have been asked to ensure the authentication of transactions and the prevention of fraud.

In 2018, the RBI also brought data storage provisions which mandated that payment-related data be stored in India.[28] A key reason for this was the Indian government's repeated difficulties in accessing cyber crime-related data stored on servers abroad. Varying legal practices further complicated this process, despite the existence of Mutual Legal Assistance Treaties. Many payment processors had opposed this provision, claiming it would disrupt their business operations.[29,30] Eventually, however, all the entities complied with the provision. The RBI will need to provide incentives, such as tax benefits, to encourage the payment industry to store data locally. This ought to be complemented by the expeditious implementation of a data-protection legal framework.

Apart from regulations, there are specific agencies which deal with various aspects of the cyber security of digital payments. The chief among these is the Institute for Development & Research in Banking Technology (IDRBT), established in 2014. It disseminates information on cyber threats in the banking and financial sector through the IB-CART, which is a one-of-its-kind mechanism for Indian banks to share threat-related information. Subsequently, in 2017, RBI also set up the ReBIT, which focuses on cyber security, research, audit and assessment of RBI-regulated entities.

The CERT-IN functions as the chief technical agency to deal with cyber threats. It operates a Botnet Cleaning and Malware Analysis Centre to detect and prevent the spread of malware infections on Indian computer networks. Moreover, it regularly brings out advisories to make individual users and organisations aware of emerging malware threats. Additionally, the industry has also taken initiatives such as the Payment Card Industry Data Security Standard[31] and SWIFT Customer Security Programme to secure inter-banking financial transactions.[32]

A dedicated CERT for the financial sector has long been awaited, which can monitor threats to the banks and other financial institutions. The government announced the plans to set up one in February 2017, but it is still discussing

Table 4.3 Regulations governing digital payments

	Title	Details
Acts and policies	Payment and Settlement Systems Act, 2007	This act provides for the regulation and supervision of payment systems in India, including electronic systems. The Ministry of Finance has proposed to amend the act, taking note of the growth in the fintech sector and the expanding role of non-banking institutions in providing payment services.
	Aadhaar (Targeted Delivery of Financial and Other Subsidies, Benefits and Services) Act, 2016	The act spells out various dimensions related to the implementation of Aadhaar-linked subsidies and other government benefit schemes. It also has provisions on the use and protection of personal and biometric information by the Unique Identification Authority.
Frameworks, guidelines and advisories	RBI Advisory on Virtual Currencies, 2013	The advisory asserts that the creation, trading or use of virtual or crypto-currencies as a medium of payment are not authorised by any central bank or monetary authority. It cautions about likely financial, operational, legal, customer protection and security-related risks from these currencies.
	NCIIPC Guidelines for the Protection of National Critical Information Infrastructure, 2015	The guidelines lay down the criteria for identifying critical information infrastructure. They enumerate 35 essential controls involving planning, implementation, operations, disaster recovery/business continuity planning and reporting and accountability for protecting critical infrastructure.
	CERT-IN Advisory CIAD-2016–0070 Securing Mobile Banking, 2016	The advisory explains various threats to mobile banking and prescribes best practices for mobile phone users to secure their phone and transactions.
	CERT-IN Advisory CIAD-2016–0069 Safeguarding Smart phones against Cyber Attacks, 2016	The advisory describes potential attack vectors for mobile phones and prescribes best practices for users to secure their phones.
	RBI Cyber Security Framework in Banks, 2016	The framework advises banks to implement various cyber-security measures for building organisational resilience, including putting in place a bank board-approved cyber security policy. It also mandates banks to report cyber incidents to the RBI's Cyber Security and Information Technology Examination cell.
	RBI Master Circular – Mobile Banking transactions in India – Operative Guidelines for Banks, 2016	This circular requires banks to put in place risk mitigation and other measures. It also mandates the use of Two-Factor Authentication.
	RBI Directive on Security and Risk Mitigation measures – Technical Audit of Prepaid Payment Instrument issuers, 2016	It advises Prepaid Payment Instrument issuers to carry out system audits and take appropriate measures against phishing attacks.

(Continued)

44 Building resilient digital payment systems

Table 4.3 (Continued)

Title	Details
RBI Policy Guidelines on Issuance and Operation of Prepaid Payment Instruments in India, 2017	The guidelines require Prepaid Payment Instrument issuers to put in place appropriate information and data-security infrastructure and systems for authentication of transactions and prevention of fraud. They also require issuers to have information security policies approved by their boards.
RBI's Basic Cyber Security Framework for Primary (Urban) Cooperative Banks, 2018	Similar to the 2016 cyber security framework for banks, this framework advises each urban cooperative bank to adopt a cyber security policy approved by its board and a cyber crisis management plan. It also mandates the banks to report all unusual cyber security incidents to the RBI's Department of Co-operative Bank Supervision.
RBI Directive on Storage of Payment System data, 2018	The directive mandates payment companies to store transaction-related data locally in India to ensure better monitoring. It says that data on the foreign parts of transactions can be stored in the relevant foreign countries.
RBI notification on prohibition on dealing in Virtual Currencies, 2018	The notification bars entities regulated by the RBI from dealing in virtual currencies or providing any related services.
Industry frameworks	
SWIFT Customer Security Programme	This programme intends to improve information sharing within the banking industry, enhance SWIFT-related tools for customers and provide a customer security control framework. The framework has mandatory and advisory security controls for SWIFT's customers.
Payment Card Industry Data Security Standard	These standards lay down technical and operational requirements for payment transactions and hardware and software used in those transactions.

Source: Gateway House research

its establishment.[33] A specialised, sectoral CERT is urgently needed to generate actionable intelligence on emerging cyber threats proactively, monitor suspicious network activity, identify threat vectors and pinpoint malicious actors.

Conclusion

India's policy push in the digital payments space, along with financial inclusion makes it an important global actor in the digital economy. However, digital payments' use can only expand if the users are confident in their security. The government and the payment industry have from time to time taken steps to patch the vulnerabilities of their systems. Still, given the ever-expanding threat canvas, they will need to be pro-active in identifying threats, sharing knowledge about them about others and educate users. Without these, it will be difficult to foster consumer trust and sustain the expansion of the digital economy.

Notes

1. This chapter is a modified version of Sameer Patil and Sagnik Chakraborty, "A Cybersecurity Agenda for India's Digital Payment Systems," Gateway House Paper no. 20, September 2019.
2. "What Is India Stack?," IndiaStack, accessed August 5, 2020, www.indiastack.org/about/.
3. "About Us: An Introduction to NPCI and Its Various Products," National Payments Corporation of India, accessed August 5, 2020, www.npci.org.in/who-we-are/about-us.
4. "RuPay Product Overview," National Payments Corporation of India, accessed November 13, 2020, www.npci.org.in/what-we-do/rupay/product-overview.
5. "About UPI API," IndiaStack, accessed August 5, 2020, www.indiastack.org/upi/.
6. Sameer Patil and Sagnik Chakraborty, "A Cybersecurity Agenda for India's Digital Payment Systems," *Gateway House*, Paper no. 20, September 2019, www.gatewayhouse.in/wp-content/uploads/2019/10/Digital-Payments_FINAL.pdf, 10.
7. "National Financial Switch Product Overview," National Payments Corporation of India, accessed December 5, 2020, www.npci.org.in/product-overview/national-financial-switch-product-overview. Figures as of December 1, 2020.
8. According to the data from the RBI, there were Rs.1,658,040 crore in digital payment transactions in September 2017, a rise of 54.32% compared to Rs.1,074,400 crore in November 2016. See, "Electronic Payment Systems: Data Dissemination (Updated as on March 06, 2018)," Reserve Bank of India, accessed December 5, 2020, www.rbi.org.in/Scripts/BS_PressReleaseDisplay.aspx?prid=39469.
9. This table is adapted from Patil and Chakraborty, *op. cit.*, 10.
10. "Internet and Mobile Association of India versus Reserve Bank of India," Supreme Court of India, accessed December 5, 2020, https://main.sci.gov.in/supremecourt/2018/19230/19230_2018_4_1501_21151_Judgement_04-Mar-2020.pdf.
11. Nalani Fraser, Jacqueline O'Leary, Vincent Cannon and Fred Plan, "APT38: Details on New North Korean Regime-Backed Threat Group," FireEye, accessed August 5, 2020, www.fireeye.com/blog/threat-research/2018/10/apt38-details-on-new-north-korean-regime-backed-threat-group.html.
12. "Mastermind behind EUR 1 Billion Cyber Bank Robbery Arrested in Spain," Europol, accessed January 26, 2020, www.europol.europa.eu/newsroom/news/mastermind-behind-eur-1-billion-cyber-bank-robbery-arrested-in-spain.
13. "Final Investigation Report Completed; Hitachi Payment Services Suffered Breach Due to Sophisticated Malware Attack in Mid-2016," Hitachi, accessed June 21, 2020, www.hitachi-payments.com/src/HPY%20Press%20Release_V9.pdf.

14 "Statement Pertaining to Press Reports on Debit Card Compromise," National Payments Corporation of India, accessed May 11, 2020, www.npci.org.in/PDF/npci/press-releases/2016/Statementpertainingtopressreportsondebitcardcompromise.pdf.
15 Patil and Chakraborty, *op. cit.*, 12.
16 "City Union Bank Cyber Attack: Successfully Retrieved/Block Money in 2 out of 3 Cases," *CNBC-TV18*, February 19, 2018, www.moneycontrol.com/news/business/companies/city-union-bank-cyber-attack-successfully-retrievedblock-money-in-2-out-of-3-cases-2510837.html.
17 Devidutta Tripathy, "India's City Union Bank CEO Says Suffered Cyber Hack Via SWIFT System," *Reuters*, February 18, 2018, www.reuters.com/article/us-city-union-bank-swift/indias-city-union-bank-ceo-says-suffered-cyber-hack-via-swift-system-idUSKCN1G20AF.
18 "Official Press Release Regarding the Unfortunate Attack on the Indian Banking Sector," Cosmos Bank, accessed May 11, 2020, www.cosmosbank.com/press-release/.
19 HT Correspondent, "2-Day Hack, Rs 94 cr Gone . . . 15 Months Later, Still No Lead in Cosmos Bank Cyber Fraud Case," *Hindustan Times*, November 16, 2019, www.hindustantimes.com/cities/15-months-later-no-lead-in-rs-94-cr-cosmos-bank-cyber-fraud-case/story-Ar6lk69HLJmBEyt9jGsx0K.html.
20 Ben Eisen, "Equifax Loses More Than $3 Billion in Market Value," *The Wall Street Journal*, September 11, 2017, https://blogs.wsj.com/moneybeat/2017/09/11/equifax-loses-more-than-3-billion-in-market-value/.
21 Brendan Pierson, "Anthem to Pay Record $115 Million to Settle U.S. Lawsuits over Data Breach," *Reuters*, June 24, 2017, www.reuters.com/article/us-anthem-cyber-settlement/anthem-to-pay-record-115-million-to-settle-u-s-lawsuits-over-data-breach-idUSKBN19E2ML.
22 Cyber security professionals, Interview by Sameer Patil, June 2017.
23 "Overview of PMGDISHA: Objective," Ministry of Electronics and Information Technology, accessed March 12, 2020, www.pmgdisha.in/about-pmgdisha/.
24 Patil and Chakraborty, *op. cit.*, 14–17.
25 "Cyber Security Framework in Banks," Reserve Bank of India, June 2, 2016, www.rbi.org.in/scripts/BS_CircularIndexDisplay.aspx?Id=10435.
26 "Comprehensive Cyber Security Framework for Primary (Urban) Cooperative Banks (UCBs): A Graded Approach," Reserve Bank of India, December 31, 2019, www.rbi.org.in/Scripts/NotificationUser.aspx?Id=11772&Moe=0.
27 "Master Direction on Issuance and Operation of Prepaid Payment Instruments," Reserve Bank of India, February 25, 2019, www.rbi.org.in/Scripts/BS_ViewMasDirections.aspx?id=11142.
28 "Storage of Payment System Data," Reserve Bank of India, April 6, 2018, www.rbi.org.in/scripts/NotificationUser.aspx?Id=11244&Mode=0.
29 Aditya Kalra, "Exclusive: U.S. Senators Urge India to Soften Data Localisation Stance," *Reuters*, October 13, 2018, https://in.reuters.com/article/india-data-localisation/exclusive-u-s-senators-urge-india-to-soften-data-localisation-stance-idINKCN1MN0CJ.
30 Vindu Goel, "U.S. Credit Card Giants Flout India's New Law on Personal Data," *The New York Times*, October 15, 2018, www.nytimes.com/2018/10/15/technology/visa-mastercard-amex-india-data-law.html.
31 "Maintaining Payment Security," Payment Standards Council, accessed December 25, 2019, www.pcisecuritystandards.org/pci_security/maintaining_payment_security.
32 "Customer Security Programme," SWIFT, accessed August 20, 2020, www.swift.com/myswift/customer-security-programme-csp.
33 Rajeev Jayaswal, "Govt Plans Cyber Security System for Financial Sector," *Hindustan Times*, August 18, 2020, www.hindustantimes.com/india-news/govt-plans-cyber-security-system/story-bHRwwBeFVGLIrA3VMmOaDO.html.

5 Murky alleys of the deep web

Introduction

The deep web is the part of the internet that is hidden beyond the open traffic of the regular internet. Typically speaking, the deep web can be any website that is not indexed by standard search engines such as Google or Yahoo, or any webpage which requires users to enter login credentials. It isn't easy to measure the data flows on the deep web, given the proliferation of websites. However, two decades ago, long before the internet had become a ubiquitous phenomenon, researchers in the United States had speculated that the deep web contained 7,500 terabytes of data, as compared to 19 terabytes on the regular internet.[1] For India, anecdotal evidence suggests approximately 70% of online traffic on the deep web.

Some parts of the deep web are accessible only through a specific encrypted browser, based on TOR technology. The TOR-enabled browser encrypts internet traffic and allows the users to remain anonymous in any online activity. While this anonymity is useful and beneficial for many users and entities, for rogue actors, this presents an opportunity to engage in criminal activities. Cyber criminals, drug traffickers and terrorist groups are increasingly utilising TOR technology and the deep web to expand their activities, earning it the notorious moniker of "dark net". This chapter examines security implications for India arising out of this misuse of the deep web.

Understanding technologies enabling the deep web

The technology which powers the deep web is "The Onion Router" technology. It was originally developed by the US Naval Research Laboratory for confidential communications, and released to the public in 2003 as free downloadable software.[2] It is so named because of its onion-like layering technique, which masks users' location data and online traffic. In 2006, some of the computer scientists involved in the development of TOR technology set up a non-profit called the TOR Project to continue further development of this technology. As the project's website explains, "The goal of onion routing was to have a way to use the internet with as much privacy as possible and the idea was to route traffic through multiple servers and encrypt it each step of the way".[3]

DOI: 10.4324/9781003152910-5

The TOR browser debuted in 2008 and, as expected, it was an instant success.[4] The technology became popular due to the growing concerns among internet users about technology companies tracking their online behaviour and intensifying state surveillance. The TOR encryption enabled these users to hide their Internet Protocol (IP) addresses – a numerical identifier assigned to a computer or device logged on the internet, making the traffic anonymous.[5] These anonymous encrypted networks are resistant to both eavesdropping and traffic analysis.[6] Fittingly, websites on the deep web use .onion as domain names, as compared to the .com or .net domains on the regular internet. Estimates from the TOR Project suggest that currently, more than 150,000 .onion domains are functional on the TOR network.[7] More than two million users connect daily to this network.[8]

It is necessary to distinguish TOR from Virtual Private Network (VPN) technology. Both TOR and VPN encrypt and anonymise the internet traffic. VPN services use a combination of dedicated connections and encryption protocols to generate virtual peer-to-peer connections. They also allow individual users to spoof their IP address, enabling them to bypass content filters. Internet Service Providers (ISPs) are unable to track internet traffic through a VPN.

In contrast, while it is difficult to do internet traffic analysis on the TOR network, ISPs and surveillance programmes can still identify TOR traffic because it passes through the TOR entry and exit nodes. Moreover, TOR anonymises the traffic by passing it through randomly selected server nodes, thereby generating random locations for its users. Just like the regular internet, users utilise several tools and technologies on the deep web, which are explained in Table 5.1.

Using the anonymity of TOR

With their promise of anonymity and encryption, TOR and the deep web have proved to be of dual use. Since the technology offers protection from security agencies' mass surveillance programmes, it has been widely used by human rights activists, political dissidents and protestors, persecuted minorities, whistle blowers and journalists.[9] For citizens living under authoritarian regimes, where internet access to news and other types of information is often censored, TOR offers unimpeded access.[10] This is, above all, true for human rights and political activists in these regimes, who may face harassment for contacting outsiders. Iranian authorities, for instance, have regularly clamped down on the increased use of TOR networks inside the country, since it allows access to Western social media platforms such as Facebook and Twitter.[11] Similarly, Russia has frequently blocked access to TOR and other anonymous networks under the pretext of cracking down on criminal activities on the dark net.[12]

TOR has also proved to be useful for investigative journalists, as they prefer to protect their sources and whistle blowers. Some people in the United States have raised concerns over the security of TOR, citing the federal government's funding for the project.[13] However, that has not stopped journalists from using it. Journalist non-profit groups such as Reporters Without Borders and the Committee to Protect Journalists, for instance, have for years used TOR to ensure greater

Table 5.1 Tools and technologies of the deep web

Technology	Tools	Details
TOR	TOR Client/Browser	TOR consists of a three-layer proxy, like layers of an onion. The browser connects at random to one of the publicly listed entry nodes, bounces that traffic through a randomly selected middle relay and exits the traffic through the third and final node.
Search engines/ Link directories	Ahima, Not Evil, Hidden Wiki, DuckDuckGo (TOR version)	Search engines trawl through the TOR network to help find the .onion domain websites. The link directories have a repository of website addresses, readily accessible to any user on the TOR network.
Communication tools	**Messengers:** TorChat, BitMessage Chat	These are decentralised, encrypted messengers that use the Tor network and encryption, based on public-key cryptography or asymmetric cryptography.
	Forums: Dread Forum, Darknet Avengers Forum	These discussion forums use encryption based on public-key cryptography or asymmetric cryptography.
	Email: TorGuard Email, CounterMail, ProtonMail TOR	These encrypted email services use TOR Network and encryption like Pretty Good Privacy (PGP). The PGP uses pairs of keys – public keys that may be disseminated widely and private keys that are known only to the owner – to encrypt and decrypt data.
Crypto-currencies	Bitcoin, Monero, Ethereum	These crypto-currencies are a preferred mode of payment for illicit transactions on the deep web.

Source: Gateway House Research[14]

privacy for its journalists.[15] TOR is also part of SecureDrop, an open-source whistle blower submission system for journalists and media organisations to accept documents from anonymous sources.[16] Some media organisations like the British Broadcasting Corporation and *The New York Times* have even launched mirror sites on TOR, to fight censorship in countries such as China.[17,18]

TOR has especially proved useful for whistle blowers and the victims of certain crimes, who wish to remain anonymous and not leave a trail of their digital communications. Similarly, political protestors have used TOR for protest mobilisation without authorities being alerted. In 2015, protestors from the Black Lives Matter movement in the United States had used TOR browsers and other encrypted messengers for getting their message across.[19]

While TOR is preferred for anonymity and privacy, it is not immune to hacking by security agencies. Examples of the crackdown by the European countries on dark net marketplaces reveal that with persistent effort, it is possible to breach the TOR network.

The dark net and cyber criminals

Criminal elements have misused the TOR technology and combined it with other widely available tools and technologies (explained earlier in Table 5.1), to operate websites which offer a cornucopia of illegal products and services.[20] Termed "dark net marketplaces" or "digital black markets", these websites had operated in the shadows for years. However, a growing portfolio of products and expanded user interest has now made them the mainstay of illegal activity on the deep web.

These marketplaces sell prohibited goods such as drugs, firearms, stolen personal and financial data, counterfeit items, snuff movies, child pornography, malware and computer viruses. Some of these marketplaces sell legal goods that were procured illegally, such as prescription drugs and consumer electronics. In addition, last year, police officials from Kerala had also noted idols and sandalwood being traded on dark net marketplaces.[21] These digital black markets also serve the extreme perversions of the human mind, such as contract killing and child pornography. Payments in these marketplaces are made in crypto-currencies such as Bitcoin, Monero and Ethereum, which have no central issuing authority and therefore enable anonymous transactions.[22]

On average, these digital black markets last for a few months to one-and-a-half years (Table 5.2). There have been some exceptions like the Silk Road marketplace, which debuted in 2011 and the US Federal Bureau of Investigation (FBI) shut it down two years later. In these two years, this marketplace had generated revenues worth USD $1.2 billion, while the various sellers who used the site had earned commissions worth approximately USD $80 million in total.[23]

Given the clandestine activities that these marketplaces engage in, user trust is paramount for them. Therefore, these marketplaces make every effort to ensure the quality of contraband and to address customers' grievances over quality, shipment and payment. Many of them also offer escrow services, where sellers receive money only after delivery of goods or services. These sites also promote the sellers, who have positive reviews from customers with verified purchases. Not surprisingly, as with any e-commerce activity, some marketplaces do dupe users, mainly by committing exit scams (failing to deliver goods and making away with escrow funds). In February 2020, one of the largest digital black markets, Apollon Market, committed an exit scam by locking out vendors and users and subsequently shutting down.[24] Similarly, in 2015, another marketplace, Evolution, had embezzled approximately USD $12 million in bitcoins from its users.[25]

Digital black markets offer easy access to stolen personal and financial data, malicious software and software vulnerability data, and computer hacking and social engineering attack tools.[26] Many of these sites facilitate the sale of stolen and forged identification documents from India, including Aadhaar cards, PAN cards, voter ID cards and passports. Black hat hackers (hackers with mala fide intentions) and organised criminal syndicates are always on the lookout for such

Table 5.2 Evolution of major dark net marketplaces and major crackdowns against them

Year	Event	Details
2011	Emergence of the Silk Road marketplace	Ross Ulbricht, a US citizen, operated it. The site forbade the sale of child pornography and weapons. It generated revenues worth USD $1.2 billion and was shut down by US FBI in 2013.
2012	Operation Adam Bomb	Executed by US Drug Enforcement Administration, the operation took down The Farmer's Market site. When taken down, it had processed USD $2.5 million in orders for illegal drugs over several years.
2013	FBI crackdown on Silk Road and the emergence of Silk Road 2.0, Dream Market and Agora	The FBI operation specifically targeted Silk Road and its owner, Ross Ulbricht, who was convicted for continuing to conduct a criminal enterprise, narcotics trafficking, money laundering and computer hacking.
		Operated by Blake Benthall, US citizen, Silk Road 2.0 recreated the Silk Road original site. The site was taken down in 2014 in Operation Onymous. Agora offered products and services similar to Silk Road. It shut itself down in 2015, fearing that potential attacks on the site might identify the site's servers and operators.
2014	Operation Onymous	A multi-nation operation involving the US FBI and Europol, it targeted 410 sites including Silk Road 2.0, whose operator Benthall was arrested, along with 17 others. Bitcoins worth USD $1 million were seized, along with €180,000 in cash, during the operation.
	Emergence of Evolution and Alpha Bay	Evolution was one of the biggest marketplaces. It closed itself down in 2015 in an exit scam; site administrators embezzled an estimated USD $12 million in bitcoins.
		At its peak, AlphaBay had 40,000 vendors selling to more than 200,000 buyers. Operated by Alexandre Cazes, a Canadian citizen, it transacted an estimated USD $1 billion since its creation in 2014. It was shut down in 2017 in Operation Bayonet.
2015	Operation Shrouded Horizon	A multi-nation crackdown led by the FBI, involving security agencies of 19 other countries, it successfully targeted the 300-member Darkode dark net forum.
	Emergence of Tochka	Tochka was smaller than its peers but gradually gained popularity. Apart from crypto-currencies, it allowed payment from PayPal accounts.
2016	Wallstreet Market	One of the most up-to-date and innovative marketplaces, Wallstreet Market, was popular with dark net users. It had deployed an award system for certain advanced security features such as multi-signature transactions, using escrow and logging in with the PGP key to encourage site users to follow security practices.

(Continued)

Table 5.2 (Continued)

Year	Event	Details
2017	Operation Bayonet	A multi-nation crackdown, it involved US FBI and Drug Enforcement Agency, along with the Dutch National Police and support from Europol. It targeted AlphaBay and Hansa, the largest marketplaces from Europe. Before shutting down, Dutch authorities took covert control of Hansa's site for a month to obtain details about vendors, users and criminal activities on the site.
	Emergence of Berlusconi	The site sold weapons including ammunition, pistols, long-range guns, explosives, hand weapons etc. It was shut down in November 2019 by Italian authorities.
2018	Operation Darkness Falls and	The two crackdowns together targeted online drug traffickers, selling fentanyl and other narcotic drugs in digital black marketplaces. One of the targeted vendors, MH4LIFE, had the highest number of verified transactions worldwide of any fentanyl vendor on the dark net.
	Operation Disarray	Under Operation Disarray, the FBI also sought to educate the users about perils of drug addiction and give training to law enforcement officials to disrupt online narcotics sales.
	Emergence of Empire marketplace	Modelled after AlphaBay, it lists more than 5,000 products, including forbidden items such as weapons.
2019–2020	Closure of Dream Market, Wallstreet Market and Tochka	American and European authorities seized Wallstreet Market in May 2019. Dream Market had become the leading marketplace after the fall of Hansa and AlphaBay. Its administrators shut it down, fearing crackdown from authorities. Tochka shut down after an exit scam in mid-2019.
	Emergence of BitBazaar	BitBazaar launched in mid-2019, selling goods and services offered by many of its predecessors. It went offline in June 2020.
	Apollon Exit Scam	One of the largest marketplaces at the time of its exit, its administrators conducted an exit scam in February 2020.

Source: Gateway House Research

documents to commit cyber crimes. Direct evidence linking these digital black markets to cyber crimes being committed in India is hard to get, as the dark net by its very nature complicates data collection efforts. However, it's clear that as more and more Indian users get on these marketplaces, India's vulnerability to cyber crimes is growing.

The outbreak of the COVID-19 pandemic has added one more dimension to these marketplaces' activities. Researchers at Georgia State University in the United States found that since late February 2020, many of these marketplaces are offering three types of COVID-19-related merchandise: protective gear, medications and services which help commit fraud.²⁷ Given that the governments were finding it difficult to procure the protective gear and medications due to high demand worldwide, the ability of these marketplaces to offer such goods certainly raised doubts over their sourcing, quality and safety. Fortunately, India has not seen such a trend.

The dark net and online drug trade

Dark net marketplaces offer drug peddlers and users a convenient medium to sell and buy narcotic substances.²⁸ Therefore, substances like cocaine, cannabis, stimulants, ecstasy, opioids and other related stuff account for two-thirds of the goods sold on these sites.²⁹ Listings such as these generated millions of dollars in monthly sales.³⁰ Online drug sales have received a further boost recently, as the lockdowns imposed due to the COVID-19 pandemic have limited users' access to physical (or "street") drug markets.

Sites like The Majestic Garden, Neptune Market and Empire have India-based vendors, offering Indian opium, Ketamine, hashish and prescription pills to customers in India and abroad. Some vendors also list Xanax bars, a synthetic drug linked to drug abuse among teens, as sourced from India.³¹ Statistics from the Narcotics Control Bureau (NCB), a central government agency in charge of drug law enforcement, give the impression that the India-related drug sales on the dark net are limited: the agency interdicted a mere four cases involving online drug purchases between 2015 and 2017.³²

But that is just the tip of the iceberg, as vendors use the most ingenious tricks to prevent law enforcement agencies from seizing their shipments of contraband. Many are also shipping the drugs in small packages, which are difficult to intercept, given the sustained focus of law enforcement agencies on larger shipments. In one such successful interdiction of smaller shipments, the NCB arrested a Delhi-based dark net vendor in February 2020, who used to disguise drug parcels while shipping sex stimulation medicines and fitness supplements.³³

The online sale of drugs is the most pernicious aspect of digital black markets for India, because it complements the well-entrenched offline smuggling syndicates that operate in India's border regions such as Punjab and the North-east.³⁴ These syndicates have used India's proximity to the two global drug-trade hubs – the "golden crescent" (Iran, Afghanistan and Pakistan) toward the west and "golden triangle" (Thailand, Laos and Myanmar) in the east, to create active illegal corridors. These are used not just for drug smuggling, but also for trafficking counterfeit Indian currency and small arms, facilitating movement of militants across borders and human trafficking, especially of women and children for commercial sexual exploitation.

The dark net and terrorist groups

Adding to the threat of expanding drug sales and cyber crimes, terrorist groups are making increased use of the dark net and digital black markets. The anonymity of the dark net offers groups such as the Daesh (also known as the Islamic State) and al-Qaeda a platform for fundraising, propaganda and easy access to weapons.³⁵ Mainstream and popular dark net marketplaces usually forbid the sale and purchase of weapons and anything related to terrorism, among other things. These marketplaces usually showcase this declaration quite prominently on their websites. However, non-mainstream marketplaces such as Berlusconi (now shut), and many stand-alone encrypted chat forums on the deep web, do sell weapons and other contraband not sold by mainstream sites. For instance, investigations in the two terrorist attacks linked to Daesh – the November 2015 Paris attack and the July 2016 Munich shooting, which together killed 140 people – revealed that weapons were purchased from such black-market sites.[36,37]

After repeatedly facing the axe from social media platforms on the regular internet like Facebook, Twitter and YouTube for posting extremist content, many terrorist groups have moved to dark net platforms and encrypted messaging apps, such as Telegram, to spread their propaganda. Daesh's virtual propaganda on dark net platforms frequently features India. This propaganda has been successful, as seen in cases of Indian youth who travelled to fight with the group in Iraq and Syria, as well as cases of Daesh-inspired lone wolf terrorists planning attacks. Cadres of the terrorist groups have also used TOR for their operational security. For instance, the Ansar Ghazwatul Hind – the al-Qaeda affiliate operating in the Kashmir Valley – has frequently advised use of VPN and TOR to avoid interception by security forces.[38] The use of these two tools exponentially increased after restrictions were put on the internet in August 2019 in the region.

Policing the deep web

With its shadowy illicit activities, the dark net and digital black markets pose a new challenge to India's national security and its nascent digital economy. India's response to this threat consists of measures at three levels: macro policy measures, law enforcement and international collaboration.

- **Macro policy measures**: as discussed in Chapter 2, at the macro level, the Indian government has already initiated several laws and regulations to fight cyber crimes and protect India's cyber space. Additionally, it has set up the I4C, which will act as the focal point to tackle cyber crimes.[39] To fight increasing instances of child pornography, the MHA has launched the National Cybercrime Reporting portal to deal with specific instances of cyber crimes against women and children, including pornography;[40]
- **Law enforcement**: at the level of law enforcement, efforts have focused on spreading awareness about the dark net and cyber crimes. Concerned departments are also providing training to their officials to identify and investigate cases of cyber fraud, extortion and other such related crimes. After intercepting the first few online shipments of narcotics in the country, the NCB has worked with other Indian security agencies to crack down on the online drug smuggling business. At the centre, this effort is coordinated at the MHA, under which several central agencies operate, including the NCB. State governments have also taken the initiative. In recent months, many state governments, including in Maharashtra, Delhi, Kerala and Telangana, have held training programmes

for their police officers. This capacity-building is an ongoing process, given the evolving nature of cyber crimes and the use of innovative methods by the criminal elements. The big gap emerging in this fight is related to the forensic skills to investigate cyber crimes and dark net activity. To address this lacuna, the Bureau of Police Research and Development, which functions as the in-house research agency for the MHA on law enforcement-related issues, has taken some initial steps by seeking solutions for monitoring the dark net and gathering threat intelligence, among others.[41] Given the gravity of the challenge posed, the government will need to create dedicated units of law enforcement officers to keep a tab on these criminal activities;

- **International collaboration**: investigating cyber crimes is a difficult task, given the limitations in the collection of evidence and multiple, sometimes foreign, jurisdictions involved. The anonymity of the dark net adds one more layer of complication into this. These factors necessitate international collaboration and, as will be seen in the next section, Western security agencies have, to some extent, tackled dark net marketplaces through cooperation. India is now also participating in such international crackdowns. For example, the NCB is part of the International Narcotics Control Board's "Operation Trance", which explicitly targets drug shipments through the mail and express courier.[42] India has also begun discussing the issue of the dark net as part of cyber security dialogues with other countries and at diplomatic forums.[43]

Global crackdown on dark net marketplaces

In recent years, American, Canadian and European law enforcement agencies have made a sustained effort to take down the leading dark net marketplaces. Their first high-profile success was the FBI's takedown of the Silk Road marketplace in 2013.[44] Since then, security agencies worldwide have had regular successes on the dark net against these marketplaces. In many cases, they employed a lemonising tactic, which involves duping buyers through exit scams or exposing anonymous transactions, to shut down these sites. Some of the recent examples of the successful crackdown are Silkkitie/Valhalla and the Wall Street Market, which were taken down by the Europol and German authorities in May 2019.[45] In addition, fearing purges, many market administrators have shut down their sites, such as the Dream Market (April 2019).[46]

However, crackdowns such as these are temporary setbacks. Sellers and users frequently move to new sites within no time, or create new ones when they fear detection. When the original Silk Road site was taken down in 2013, in no time, a new avatar, Silk Road 2.0, appeared. When it was taken down in October 2014, within hours, its spawns went online, some of them even selling items eschewed by Silk Road, such as child pornography.[47] Besides, these newer iterations have learned from the experience and mistakes of their predecessors, becoming tougher and more complex to track and crack.

A study from the United Nations Office on Drugs and Crime had revealed that more than one-half of customers who had used closed websites to purchase narcotics did not consider themselves to have been affected by these regular crackdowns; just 15% of the clients were deterred, and only 9% completely stopped using dark net sites.[48] The shadowy players of the deep web are clearly resilient in their illegal activities.

Conclusion

The challenge of the dark net is only going to deepen further, as cyber criminals develop newer methods to carry out cyber crimes. Building capacity and joining hands with other law enforcement agencies worldwide are the two definite ways by which Indian law enforcement agencies can tackle this threat. They should also collaborate with responsible commercial stakeholders, like crypto-currency exchanges and VPN service providers, to keep track of these illicit transactions. Ultimately, law enforcement agencies will need to show the same kind of "out-of-box" thinking as the operators of these shadowy sites have demonstrated.

Notes

1 Michael K. Bergman, "White Paper: The Deep Web: Surfacing Hidden Value," *The Journal of Electronic Publishing* 7, no. 1 (August 2001), https://doi.org/10.3998/3336451.0007.104.
2 Roger Dingledine, Nick Mathewson and Paul Syverson, "Tor: The Second-Generation Onion Router," SSYM'04: Proceedings of the 13th Conference on USENIX Security Symposium 13, August 2004, www.usenix.org/legacy/publications/library/proceedings/sec04/tech/full_papers/dingledine/dingledine.pdf.
3 "History," TOR Project, accessed June 15, 2020, www.torproject.org/about/history/.
4 "New Tor Distribution for Testing: Tor Browser Bundle," Tor Project, accessed June 15, 2020, https://lists.torproject.org/pipermail/tor-talk/2008-January/007837.html.
5 Apart from TOR, other available but less-widely used network encryption technologies are I2P (Invisible Internet Project/Garlic Router) and Freenet.
6 Paul Syverson, "Onion Routing for Resistance to Traffic Analysis," Proceedings DARPA Information Survivability Conference and Exposition, 2003, 2: 108–110.
7 "Onion Services," TOR Metrics, accessed June 15, 2020, https://metrics.torproject.org/hidserv-dir-onions-seen.html.
8 "Users," TOR Metrics, accessed June 15, 2020, https://metrics.torproject.org/userstats-relay-country.html.
9 Aditi Kumar and Eric Rosenbach, "The Truth about the Dark Web," *Finance and Development* 56, no. 3 (September 2019): 22–25.
10 David Omand, "The Dark Net: Policing the Internet's Underworld," *World Policy Journal* 32, no. 4 (Winter 2015–16): 75–82.
11 Lorenzo Franceschi-Bicchierai, "Iran Is Trying to Block Tor," *Vice*, March 5, 2015, www.vice.com/en_us/article/ae3am5/iran-is-trying-to-block-tor.
12 BBC, "Russian Intelligence 'Targets Tor Anonymous Browser'," July 22, 2019, www.bbc.com/news/technology-49071225.
13 Brian Fung, "The Feds Pay for 60 Percent of Tor's Development: Can Users Trust It?," *The Washington Post*, September 6, 2013, www.washingtonpost.com/news/the-switch/wp/2013/09/06/the-feds-pays-for-60-percent-of-tors-development-can-users-trust-it/?arc404=true.
14 This table is adapted from Sameer Patil, "Partnering for Prosperity: India-Canada Collaboration to Curb Digital Black Markets," CIGI-Gateway House Canada-India Track

1.5 Dialogue, no. 2 (2019), www.gatewayhouse.in/wp-content/uploads/2019/02/Canada-India-Paper-no-2_0.pdf.
15 "Reporters Without Borders and Torservers.net, Partners Against Online Surveillance and Censorship," Reporters Without Borders, accessed August 19, 2020, https://rsf.org/en/news/reporters-without-borders-and-torserversnet-partners-against-online-surveillance-and-censorship.
16 "Tor at the Heart: SecureDrop," Tor Blog, accessed August 19, 2020, https://blog.torproject.org/tor-heart-securedrop.
17 Runa Sandvik, "The New York Times Is Now Available as a Tor Onion Service," *NYT Open*, October 27, 2017, https://open.nytimes.com/https-open-nytimes-com-the-new-york-times-as-a-tor-onion-service-e0d0b67b7482.
18 BBC, "BBC News Launches 'Dark Web' Tor Mirror," October 23, 2019, www.bbc.com/news/technology-50150981.
19 Alex Altman, "Black Lives Matter," *Time*, December 31, 2015, https://time.com/time-person-of-the-year-2015-runner-up-black-lives-matter/.
20 See n. 10.
21 Economic Times, "Tracing Dark Web Crimes a Big Challenge for Kerala Police," September 23, 2019, https://government.economictimes.indiatimes.com/news/secure-india/tracing-dark-web-crimes-a-big-challenge-for-kerala-police/71258534.
22 Michael Chertoff, "A Public Policy Perspective of the Dark Web," *Journal of Cyber Policy* 2, no. 1 (2017): 26–38.
23 "Manhattan U.S. Attorney Announces Seizure of Additional $28 Million Worth of Bitcoins Belonging to Ross William Ulbricht, Alleged Owner and Operator of "Silk Road" Website," Federal Bureau of Investigation, United States Department of Justice, accessed June 15, 2020, https://archives.fbi.gov/archives/newyork/press-releases/2013/manhattan-u.s.-attorney-announces-seizure-of-additional-28-million-worth-of-bitcoins-belonging-to-ross-william-ulbricht-alleged-owner-and-operator-of-silk-road-website.
24 "Trends in the Availability and Type of Drugs Sold on the Internet Via Cryptomarkets, January 2019–January 2020," National Drug & Alcohol Research Centre, University of New South Wales, accessed June 15, 2020, https://ndarc.med.unsw.edu.au/resource-analytics/test-page-trends-availability-and-type-drugs-sold-internet-cryptomarkets-january.
25 Nicky Woolf, "Bitcoin 'Exit Scam': Deepweb Market Operators Disappear with $12m," *The Guardian*, March 18, 2015, www.theguardian.com/technology/2015/mar/18/bitcoin-deepweb-evolution-exit-scam-12-million-dollars.
26 Abdullah M. Algarni and Yashwant K. Malaiya, "Software Vulnerability Markets: Discoverers and Buyers," *International Journal of Computer, Electrical, Automation, Control and Information Engineering* 8, no. 3 (2014): 480–489.
27 David Maimon, "Sketchy Darknet Websites Are Taking Advantage of the COVID-19 Pandemic: Buyer Beware," *The Conversation*, August 19, 2020, https://theconversation.com/sketchy-darknet-websites-are-taking-advantage-of-the-covid-19-pandemic-buyer-beware-143237.
28 One recent trend suggests that given the spate of exit scams and trust issues, many of the drug users and sellers are also shifting to social media platforms, which, while not being secure, do offer anonymity. Drug sales on social media platforms like Instagram are perceived as an intermediary option between the drug peddlers on the street and digital black markets. See Leah Moyle, Andrew Childs, Ross Coomber and Monica J. Barratt, "#Drugsforsale: An Exploration of the Use of Social Media and Encrypted Messaging Apps to Supply and Access Drugs," *International Journal of Drug Policy* 63 (January 2019): 101–110.
29 See n. 24.
30 As per one study done by the RAND Corporation, in the Netherlands alone, these drug sales generated a total monthly revenue of $14.2 million. See Kristy Kruithof, Judith

Aldridge, David Décary Hétu, Megan Sim, Elma Dujso and Stijn Hoorens, "Internet-Facilitated Drugs Trade: An Analysis of the Size, Scope and the Role of the Netherlands," *RAND Corporation*, 2016, www.rand.org/pubs/research_reports/RR1607.html.

31 Sameer Patil, "Policing Digital Black Markets," *Gateway House*, September 26, 2019, www.gatewayhouse.in/digital-black-markets/.

32 Annual reports for 2015, 2016 and 2017 of the Narcotics Control Bureau, Ministry of Home Affairs, Government of India available at http://narcoticsindia.nic.in/.

33 Jignasa Sinha, "Delhi: 21-Year-Old Drug Dealer Operating through the 'Dark Web' Arrested," *The Indian Express*, February 10, 2020, https://indianexpress.com/article/cities/delhi/21-yr-old-drug-dealer-operating-through-the-dark-web-arrested-6259629/.

34 Sameer Patil, "Punjab's Unshakable Drug Smuggling Networks," *Gateway House*, April 17, 2018, www.gatewayhouse.in/punjabs-drug-smuggling/.

35 Gabriel Weimann, "Terrorist Migration to the Dark Web," *Perspectives on Terrorism* 10, no. 3 (2016): 40–44.

36 Ruth Bender and Christopher Alessi, "Munich Shooter Likely Bought Reactivated Pistol on Dark Net," *Wall Street Journal*, July 24, 2016, www.wsj.com/articles/munich-shooter-bought-recommissioned-pistol-on-dark-net-1469366686.

37 DW, "Report: Evidence Paris Attack Weapons Shipped from Germany," November 27, 2015, www.dw.com/en/report-evidence-paris-attack-weapons-shipped-from-germany/a-18879149.

38 "Ansar Ghazwatul Hind Security Guidelines for the Mujahideen in Kashmir," *Al-Hurr Media*, November 2018.

39 "Details about Indian Cybercrime Coordination Centre (I4C) Scheme," Ministry of Home Affairs, Government of India, accessed August 19, 2020, www.mha.gov.in/division_of_mha/cyber-and-information-security-cis-division/Details-about-Indian-Cybercrime-Coordination-Centre-I4C-Scheme.

40 "National Cyber Crime Reporting Portal," Ministry of Home Affairs, Government of India, accessed August 19, 2020, https://cybercrime.gov.in/.

41 "Request for R&D Proposals on Cyber Crime/Security/Digital Forensic Solutions," Bureau of Police Research & Development and National Cyber Research & Innovation Centre, Ministry of Home Affairs, Government of India, accessed June 15, 2020, https://bprd.nic.in/WriteReadData/Orders/RFP%20final.pdf.

42 "Major Tramadol Trafficking Network Dismantled under INCB's 'Operation Trance'," International Narcotics Control Bureau, accessed June 15, 2020, www.incb.org/incb/en/news/press-releases/2020/major-tramadol-trafficking-network-dismantled-under-incbs-operation-trance.html.

43 PTI, "Darknet Misuse for Drug Crimes Discussed in BRICS Meet Attended by India: MHA," *The Economic Times*, August 16, 2020, https://economictimes.indiatimes.com/news/politics-and-nation/darknet-misuse-for-drug-crimes-discussed-in-brics-meet-attended-by-indiamha/articleshow/77572061.cms?from=mdr.

44 Jose Pagliery, "FBI Shuts Down Online Drug Market Silk Road," *CNN Business*, October 2, 2013, https://money.cnn.com/2013/10/02/technology/silk-road-shut-down/index.html.

45 "Double Blow to Dark Web Marketplaces," Europol, accessed June 15, 2020, www.europol.europa.eu/newsroom/news/double-blow-to-dark-web-marketplaces.

46 Catalin Cimpanu, "Top Dark Web Marketplace Will Shut Down Next Month," *ZDNet*, March 26, 2019, www.zdnet.com/article/top-dark-web-marketplace-will-shut-down-next-month/.

47 "Post Silk Road: Another Online Drug Den Now Dominates the DarkNet," Digital Citizens Alliance, accessed June 15, 2020, https://media.gractions.com/314A5A5A9ABBBBC5E3BD824CF47C46EF4B9D3A76/2251410a-790a-459c-a48a-6a4fd7dcfb88.pdf.

48 "World Drug Report 2018," United Nations Office on Drugs and Crime, accessed August 19, 2020, www.unodc.org/wdr2018.

6 India's lead in cyber diplomacy

Introduction

As seen in the previous chapters, advances in information and communication technologies have created opportunities as well as challenges for humankind. The constant evolution of cyber threats, along with their trans-border nature, has made cyber security and related digital issues a critical area of international collaboration. The urgency of such collaboration is reinforced by the anarchic nature of cyber space, which has no formal, comprehensive governance framework. Repeated attempts to regulate it have faced setbacks due to the differing visions of major powers and developing countries.

In this global backdrop of flux, India, as an emerging economy with a large IT industry and a well-established technological base, has been reasonably active on digital and cyber issues at the international level and multilateral forums. Spearheaded by the MEA and the MEITY, this global engagement has broadly spanned creation of global cyber norms, managing internet governance and the bilateral cyber diplomacy, including capacity-building programmes with like-minded countries. These efforts are merging into an Indian vision for global cyber governance. If India continues on this path, it has the potential to resonate with the developing countries that are just starting on the path of national digital transformation.

India's initial engagement on cyber issues at the global level

Since its independence, India has had a history of active participation in the shaping of global norms. This was evident in its advocacy of decolonisation and universal nuclear disarmament. This advocacy was an important expression of India's commitment to multilateralism, and an attempt by then-Prime Minister Jawaharlal Nehru to carve out an alternate conception of world order for the newly independent countries of Asia and Africa, beyond the Cold War rivalry between the two superpowers. On the issues of arms control and disarmament, India often found itself at odds with the superpowers, and India did not become part of the important arms control agreements, such as the Treaty on the Non-Proliferation of Nuclear Weapons, due to lack of sufficient commitment by the major powers towards disarmament. But this oddity did not diminish New Delhi's enthusiasm

DOI: 10.4324/9781003152910-6

to support and promote efforts towards the creation of regimes for emerging technologies, with implications for international security. Similar concerns guided its approach to cyber and digital issues.

India's engagement with digital and cyber issues began immediately when the use of the internet expanded in India in the late 1990s. The World Wide Web offered ordinary Indians an opportunity to connect with the outside world, at a time when their access to the outside information was still restricted. Given the interconnected nature of this information superhighway, many countries around the world led by the Western powers were eager to put in place a regime to control this emerging "global commons". India was only eager to join these countries. This eagerness notwithstanding, India mostly adopted a low profile in multilateral forums such as the International Telecommunications Union (ITU) and initial iterations of the World Summit on the Information Society (WSIS), possibly because Indian policymakers were grasping nuances of the issues at hand.[1] In the first two phases of the WSIS, in Geneva (2003) and Tunis (2005), India supported other countries' appeal for greater use of information and communication technologies for economic development.[2]

India's contribution in shaping global cyber norms

The creation of the GGE by the UN in 2004 provided India with the opportunity to be part of the group shaping the norms for state behaviour in cyber space. Since then, India has been part of the four GGE processes, and is also part of the 2019–2021 GGE.[3] Faced with mounting attacks from hostile neighbours and their proxies, India has put cyber security at the core of its concerns. Thus, it has repeatedly highlighted the necessity of developing a common understanding of responsible state behaviour, including on matters of attribution and cyber terrorism. It has also emphasised the adoption of confidence-building measures by states to address cyber threats and supported the "right to self-defence" against state-sponsored cyber attacks.[4] However, evolving consensus on these issues has proved difficult, as was evident from the collapse of the fifth GGE process in 2017.[5] On cyber terrorism, India is also a signatory to the Christchurch Call to Action of May 2019, which came in the wake of the terrorist attack in Christchurch, New Zealand on 15 March 2019.[6] The Call lays down voluntary commitments for governments and online service providers to tackle terrorist and violent extremist content in the digital space.

Like its counterparts in the global south, India's concerns at the GGE and other multilateral forums have reflected both the "pull" of economic development (beneficiary of the free flow of data) and the "pressure" of national security (concern with ever-increasing cyber attacks).[7] As a result, its diplomacy has been a combination of multilateralism and sovereignty – much like its advocacy of nuclear disarmament, where it advocated for a universal disarmament regime, but resisted giving up its right to develop nuclear weapons until the existing nuclear powers committed to genuine disarmament measures.

Though it has broadly identified with the Western arguments on cyber stability, Indian diplomacy has also carved out its positions on critical issues, distinct from the Western bloc. This is evident from its formulations on data localisation and digital trade issues, which are closer to the Chinese and Russian positions than the American stance. Its position on data localisation echoes the data sovereignty argument that states should have the sovereign right to govern and manage the data of their citizens and within their territory or jurisdiction.[8] Thus, despite being a votary of multilateralism, India stayed out of the Osaka Track for Data Governance at the G20 Summit in 2019.[9] Likewise, it has opposed the Budapest Convention on Cybercrime.[10] On digital trade, it has resisted Western countries' pressures to join the negotiations on e-commerce at the World Trade Organization (WTO).[11] Moreover, in 2018, India voted for competing proposals from the United States (for setting up the 2019–2021 GGE) and Russia (to establish an Open-Ended Working Group in parallel with the GGE), which suggested that it was exploring options which would best contribute to the shaping of cyber norms.[12]

These dynamics have lent India the position of being a legitimate representative of developing countries for shaping cyber norms. Even as India's concerns in this arena reflect those of the developing countries, with a focus on using information and communication technologies for national socio-economic developments, a specific driver for its engagement has been to ensure an unimpeded growth of its IT sector, which had bestowed India a global profile, particularly in software exports.[13]

In addition to the GGE, India has also been parts of efforts such as the UN Secretary General's High-Level Panel on Digital Cooperation, where it was represented by Ambassador Amandeep Singh Gill, who served as an ex-officio member. The panel in its report had given multiple ideas to shape global cyber norms, including the creation of a global mechanism to foster cooperation.[14] India has also supported non-governmental efforts such as the consultations on the Tallinn Manual (The Hague, February 2016), Global Conference on Cyber Space (hosted in New Delhi in November 2017) and the Global Commission on the Stability of Cyberspace, which has worked to develop cyber norms.[15,16,17]

India and the issue of internet governance

Since the WSIS process, India has sought an equitable distribution of power for all countries, including developing ones, in the internet governance ecosystem. According to Anja Kovacs, there were two defining features of India's initial position on internet governance.[18] The first was that India repeatedly stressed the multi-stakeholder model when it stated that the management of internet governance has to be "representative, democratic, transparent and accountable, involving governments and other stakeholders as per the Tunis Agenda". Secondly, it highlighted that appropriate legal and international frameworks need to be created for this internet governance.

India's position on this issue has seen significant evolution. An overview of Indian engagement on this issue demonstrates a strong belief in the multi-stakeholder model over the last few years, after the initial support for a state-centric approach to deal with internet governance issues. In 2011, India put forward the proposal to establish the UN Committee on Internet-related Policies (CIRP), with states as members and non-government entities such as the private sector, civil society and inter-governmental organisations in an advisory role.[19] The proposal for CIRP was based on proceedings of an earlier meeting of the India, Brazil and South Africa grouping at a multi-stakeholder meeting on internet governance.[20] However, India's plan was criticised as "an anti-multi-stakeholder move", since it proposed a dominant position for the state actors.[21]

This vacillation between multilateralism and multi-stakeholderism – what some analysts called "nuanced multilateralism"[22] – settled in favour of the latter in 2015, when India explicitly endorsed the American proposal for the multi-stakeholder model for managing the Internet Corporation for Assigned Names and Numbers (ICANN), which manages the global internet infrastructure.[23] The Indian position, therefore, went against the Russian and Chinese approach, which preferred making ICANN, a multilateral body, be controlled by national governments. Yet India has also attempted to convince the Russian and Chinese side to support the multi-stakeholder model – and with some success. The Brazil, Russia, India, China and South Africa (BRICS) grouping, through successive BRICS declarations between 2015–2018, had emphasised the need to involve relevant stakeholders in the evolution and functioning of the internet and its governance.[24]

Cyber dialogues with like-minded countries

As noted in Chapter 2, the MEA established Cyber Diplomacy as an independent division within the ministry to focus on cyber issues. This gave a significant impetus to New Delhi's bilateral engagements and participation in multilateral forums dealing with cyber issues (Table 6.1). In the last few years, India has held cyber dialogues with more than 15 countries and two organisations (the European Union and Association of Southeast Asian Nations).[25] These have included wide-ranging exchanges on best cyber security practices, capacity-building towards the protection of

Table 6.1 India's cyber interactions

Bilateral cyber dialogues	Australia, Egypt, France, Japan, Netherlands, New Zealand, UK, United States, ASEAN, European Union
Bilateral cyber agreements and MoUs	Bangladesh, Brazil, Bulgaria, Canada, China, Columbia, Estonia, France, Finland, Germany, Ireland, Israel, Japan, Jordan, Malaysia, Palestine, Portugal, Qatar, Serbia, Singapore, South Africa, South Korea, Vietnam, Tanzania, Tunisia
CERT-India's foreign collaborations	South Korea, Japan, Mauritius, United States, Australia, Malaysia, Singapore, UK, United States, Uzbekistan, Vietnam, Bangladesh, Estonia, Finland, Seychelles, Morocco, Israel
Participation in technical forums	ITU's International Multilateral Partnership Against Cyber Threats, INTERPOL Global Complex for Innovation, Forum of Incident Response and Security Teams (Group of CERTs), Asia Pacific CERT, Anti-Phishing Working Group international coalition

Source: Gateway House Research

critical information infrastructure, tackling threats posed by cyber crimes and cyber terrorism.

One major trend observable in the bilateral cyber engagements is that cyber security cooperation has been a sub-set of broader security collaboration. Therefore, India has found it easier to evolve such cooperation with those countries with whom it already had a well-established security partnership. One notable instance of this has been the cooperation with the United States. Since the signing of the framework agreement for defence cooperation and Mumbai attacks of 2008, defence trade, intelligence-sharing and counter-terrorism cooperation between the two countries has flourished.[26] Building on this deep collaboration, both countries signed the "Framework for India-US Cyber Relationship for enhanced cooperation in the field of ICT and Cyber Security" in 2016, which paved the way for further cooperation to tackle multiple shared cyber threats and sync approaches at the global level on issues such as internet governance.[27]

Three other notable instances are India's collaborations with France, Australia and Japan. After the United States, France is the only country with whom India has signed such a comprehensive framework for cooperation.[28] India is expected to benefit from French expertise in emerging technologies such as Artificial Intelligence (AI) and quantum computing. Another promising partnership is with Australia, where apart from AI and quantum computing, cooperation on robotics is expected to be beneficial for both sides.[29] In addition, India's cyber capacity-building programmes with the countries in the Indo-Pacific align well with Australia's cyber diplomacy, under which it has engaged the Indo-Pacific countries in capacity-building on cyber crime prevention and prosecution.[30] Another collaboration which has potential in this domain is India's agreement with Japan, where both sides have agreed to work together on 5G technology and critical information infrastructure.[31] Moreover, combined with Australia and the United States, the agreement with Japan shows the potential of the "Quadrilateral Security Initiative" to act together on cyber security issues.

Efforts for cyber capability-building in the Indo-Pacific and Africa

The key to tackle cyber threats and regulate cyber affairs is building capacity. However, this is easier said than done, as many developing countries lack the necessary know-how and monetary resources to fight cyber threats. These countries require external assistance in building their capacity. Recognising this need, India, just like other digital powers, harnessing its IT expertise, has stepped up its efforts to share its cyber knowledge with developing countries in the Indo-Pacific and Africa. In recent years, India is helping countries like Bangladesh, Tunisia and Vietnam through bilateral agreements and MoUs. It has also helped by setting up Centres of Excellence and Institutes of Technology in various countries.

Additionally, multilateral forums such as the Global Forum on Cyber Expertise (GFCE, of which India is a founding member) are also facilitating India's engagement with other developing countries for capacity-building, sharing of best practices and regular exchange on cyber security issues.[32] For example, under the GFCE, India has shared its "Cyber Surakshit Bharat Initiative", which seeks to spread awareness about cyber security among the Chief Information Security Officers and frontline IT staff.[33,34]

This capacity-building also has a strong training element as part of the Indian Technical and Economic Cooperation (ITEC) programme, implemented by the MEA. Many government institutions, such as the C-DAC and the Sardar Vallabhbhai Patel National Police Academy, along with academic institutions such as the Gujarat Forensic Sciences University and Indian Institute of Technology-Kanpur, have trained the ITEC participants in various aspects of cyber security.[35,36]

Through CERT-IN and its law enforcement agencies, India also participates in various technical forums, such as the International Multilateral Partnership Against Cyber Threats – the technical arm of the ITU. These forums deal with technical issues such as cyber criminal investigations, cyber forensics, threat attack vectors etc.

Promoting the digital economy

In 2016, at the G20 summit at Hangzhou, China created the Digital Economy Task Force to develop cooperation in the digital domain.[37] As seen in the chapter on digital payments, India has implemented multiple domestic initiatives, aimed at financial inclusion, data protection and cyber security of payment systems. Also, India has used innovations such as IndiaStack to expand the usage of digital payment systems. India's experiences as a developing economy are an important contributor to the expansion of the digital economy. They have determined its approach to e-commerce and digital trade issues at the WTO and other multilateral forums, including on issues of data governance. This has had greater resonance with developing countries that are adjusting to the rapid technological changes to harness it for domestic development.

Conclusion

As characterised by the Canadian economist Rohinton Medhora, the world today is divided into three incompatible blocs: the state-centric China bloc, the firm-centric US bloc and the individual-centric General Data Protection Regime zone of the European Union. India, with nearly 700 million internet users and an emerging digital economy, does not align itself completely with any of these blocs. Therefore, it is uniquely placed to shape the outcome of the global debate on many emerging cyber security and digital issues. Additionally, since India emphasises the multi-stakeholder approach, it should also consult businesses, civil society organisations and academia for input informing its policy positions at the multilateral fora. Frigid great power relations may undermine efforts to shape a regime to govern cyber space, but India, through its active cyber diplomacy, can pivot developing countries to engage in international cooperation and therefore contribute to the shaping of global norms.

Notes

1 Sandeep Bhardwaj, "Security in Cyberspace: India's Multilateral Efforts," in *Shaping the Emerging World: India and the Multilateral Order*, eds. W. P. Singh Sidhu, Pratap Bhanu Mehta and Bruce Jones (Washington: Brookings Institution Press, 2013), 219–221.
2 Subimal Bhattacharjee, "Cyber Diplomacy: India's March," *Observer Research Foundation*, September 5, 2013, www.orfonline.org/research/cyber-diplomacy-indias-march/.
3 Arindrajit Basu, "India's Role in Global Cyber Policy Formulation," *Lawfare*, November 7, 2019, www.lawfareblog.com/indias-role-global-cyber-policy-formulation.
4 Hannes Ebert, "Hacked IT Superpower: How India Secures Its Cyberspace as a Rising Digital Democracy," *India Review* 19, no. 4 (October 2020): 376–413.
5 Adam Segal, "The Development of Cyber Norms at the United Nations Ends in Deadlock. Now What?," *Council on Foreign Relations*, June 29, 2017, www.cfr.org/blog/development-cyber-norms-united-nations-ends-deadlock-now-what.
6 "Christchurch Call to Eliminate Terrorist and Violent Extremist Content Online," The Ministry of Foreign Affairs and Trade, accessed November 26, 2020, www.christchurchcall.com/call.html.
7 Sameer Patil, "India's Lead on Cyber Space Governance," *Gateway House*, August 15, 2018, www.gatewayhouse.in/india-cyber-space-governance/.
8 See n. 3.
9 Bhaswati Mukherjee, "India at Osaka: Strong and Balanced," *India Perspectives* 3 (2019), www.indiaperspectives.gov.in/en_US/india-at-osaka-strong-and-balanced/
10 Sameer Patil, Purvaja Modak, Kunal Kulkarni and Aditya Phatak, "India-EU Cooperation on Cyber Security and Data Protection," in *Moving Forward EU-India Relations: The Significance of the Security Dialogues*, eds. Nicola Casarini, Stefania Benaglia and Sameer Patil (Rome: Edizioni Nuova Cultura, 2017), 47–77.
11 For a detailed look at domestic and international dimensions of India's position on e-commerce issues, see Ambika Khanna, "A Critique of India's Draft National e-Commerce Policy," *Gateway House*, April 4, 2019, www.gatewayhouse.in/india-e-commerce-policy/.
12 Arindrajit Basu and Elonnai Hickok, "Cyber Security and External Affairs: A Memorandum for India," *The Centre for Internet and Society*, November 30, 2018, https://cis-india.org/internet-governance/files/cyberspace-and-external-affairs.
13 Asoke Mukerji, "International Cooperation on Cyber Space: India's Role," National Academy of Customs, Indirect Taxes and Narcotics, Faridabad, April 4, 2018, www.mea.gov.in/distinguished-lectures-detail.htm?743.
14 "The Age of Digital Interdependence," Report of the UN Secretary-General's High-Level Panel on Digital Cooperation, accessed November 26, 2020, www.un.org/en/pdfs/DigitalCooperation-report-for%20web.pdf.
15 Michael N. Schmitt (ed.), *Tallinn Manual 2.0 on the International Law Applicable to Cyber Operations* (Cambridge: Cambridge University Press, 2017).
16 Samir Saran, "A Reluctant Digital Power Emerges From the Shadows," *The Wire*, December 22, 2016, https://thewire.in/diplomacy/emergence-reluctant-digital-power.
17 "The Commission," Global Commission on the Stability of Cyberspace, accessed June 15, 2020, https://cyberstability.org/about/.
18 Anja Kovacs, "Is a Reconciliation of Multistakeholderism and Multilateralism in Internet Governance Possible? India at NETmundial," *Internet Democracy Project*, https://internetdemocracy.in/reports/india-at-netmundial/.
19 "India's Statement Proposing UN Committee for Internet-Related Policy," The Centre for Internet and Society, accessed November 26, 2020, https://cis-india.org/internet-governance/blog/india-statement-un-cirp.
20 Cherian Samuel, "Cyber Security: Global, Regional and Local Dynamics," *IDSA* Monograph Series, no. 42 (December 2014), 32.

21 Sunil Abraham, Mukta Batra, Geetha Hariharan, Swaraj Barooah and Akriti Bopanna, "India's Contribution to the Internet Governance Debates," *NLUD Journal of Legal Studies* 5 (2018): 1–25.
22 *Op. cit.*
23 "Indian Government Declares Support for Multistakeholder Model of Internet Governance at ICANN53," ICANN, June 22, 2015, www.icann.org/resources/press-material/release-2015-06-22-en.
24 See n. 7.
25 "Annual Report 2019–20," Ministry of External Affairs, accessed November 26, 2020, www.mea.gov.in/Uploads/PublicationDocs/32489_AR_Spread_2020_new.pdf, 290.
26 Sameer Patil, "Deepening India-U.S. Defence Partnership," *Gateway House*, November 5, 2020, www.gatewayhouse.in/india-u-s-defence-ties/.
27 "Framework for the U.S.-India Cyber Relationship," U.S. Embassy & Consulates in India, August 30, 2016, https://in.usembassy.gov/framework-u-s-india-cyber-relationship/.
28 Sagnik Chakraborty, "Indo-French Digital Partnership," *Gateway House*, September 12, 2019, www.gatewayhouse.in/digital-partnership/.
29 "Australia and India Agree New Partnership on Cyber and Critical Technology," Minister for Foreign Affairs, June 4, 2020, www.foreignminister.gov.au/minister/marise-payne/media-release/australia-and-india-agree-new-partnership-cyber-and-critical-technology.
30 Sameer Patil, "An Amplified India-Australia Security," *Gateway House*, June 27, 2019, www.gatewayhouse.in/india-australia-security/.
31 Rezaul H. Laskar, "India, Japan Finalise Key Cyber-Security Deal to Boost Cooperation on 5G, AI," *Hindustan Times*, October 7, 2020, www.hindustantimes.com/india-news/india-japan-finalise-key-cyber-security-deal-to-boost-cooperation-on-5g-ai/story-WCMa9En3NFPkQMWClGNFJI.html.
32 Mirko Hohmann, Alexander Pirang and Thorsten Benner, "Advancing Cybersecurity Capacity Building: Implementing a Principle-Based Approach," *Global Public Policy Institute*, March 2017, www.gppi.net/media/Hohmann__Pirang__Benner__2017__Advancing_Cybersecurity_Capacity_Building.pdf, 30.
33 "MEITY Launches Cyber Surakshit Bharat to Strengthen Cybersecurity," Ministry of Electronics & Information Technology, accessed January 19, 2018, https://pib.gov.in/PressReleaseIframePage.aspx?PRID=1517238.
34 Cherian Samuel, "Bringing Capacity Building in Cybersecurity to the Fore," *Manohar Parrikar Institute for Defence Studies and Analyses*, December 26, 2018, https://idsa.in/idsacomments/capacity-building-cybersecurity-to-the-fore_csamuel_261218.
35 "Indian Technical and Economic Cooperation Programme," Centre for Development of Advanced Computing, accessed June 15, 2020, www.cdac.in/index.aspx?id=print_page&print=edu_et_E_IPC_DACMohali
36 See n. 25, 98, 122 and 211.
37 "G20 Leaders' Communique Hangzhou Summit," Ministry of Foreign Affairs, People's Republic of China, September 4–5, 2016, www.g20chn.com/xwzxEnglish/sum_ann/201609/t20160906_3397.html.

Bibliography

Basu, Arindrajit. "India's Role in Global Cyber Policy Formulation." *Lawfare*, November 7, 2019. www.lawfareblog.com/indias-role-global-cyber-policy-formulation.

Basu, Arindrajit and Elonnai Hickok. "Cyber Security and External Affairs: A Memorandum for India." *The Centre for Internet and Society*, November 30, 2018. https://cis-india.org/internet-governance/files/cyberspace-and-external-affairs.

Bhardwaj, Sandeep. "Security in Cyberspace: India's Multilateral Efforts." Essay. In *Shaping the Emerging World: India and the Multilateral Order*, edited by W. P. Singh Sidhu, Bruce Jones and Pratap Bhanu Mehta, 217–236. Washington, DC: Brookings Institution Press, 2013.

Bronk, Christopher and Eneken Tikk-Ringas. "The Cyber Attack on Saudi Aramco." *Survival* 55, no. 2 (April–May 2013): 81–96.

Chen, Thomas M. *Cyberterrorism after Stuxnet*. Carlisle, PA: Strategic Studies Institute, US Army War College, 2014.

Chertoff, Michael. "A Public Policy Perspective of the Dark Web." *Journal of Cyber Policy* 2, no. 1 (2017): 26–38.

Department of Economic Affairs, Ministry of Finance. "Report of the Working Group for setting up of Computer Emergency Response Team in the financial sector (CERT-Fin)." Accessed June 15, 2010. http://dea.gov.in/sites/default/files/Press-CERT-Fin%20Report.pdf.

Ebert, Hannes. "Hacked IT Superpower: How India Secures Its Cyberspace as a Rising Digital Democracy." *India Review* 19, no. 4 (October 2020): 376–413.

FireEye. "Russia's APT28 Strategically Evolves Its Cyber Operations." Accessed June 15, 2020. www.fireeye.com/current-threats/apt-groups/rpt-apt28.html.

FireEye. "Threat Research: APT 30 and the Mechanics of a Long-Running Cyber Espionage Operation." Accessed June 15, 2020. www2.fireeye.com/rs/fireye/images/rpt-apt30.pdf.

Fraser, Nalani, Jacqueline O'Leary, Vincent Cannon and Fred Plan. "APT38: Details on New North Korean Regime-Backed Threat Group." Accessed August 5, 2020. www.fireeye.com/blog/threat-research/2018/10/apt38-details-on-new-north-korean-regime-backed-threat-group.html.

Hannas, William C., James Mulvenon and Anna B. Puglist. *Chinese Industrial Espionage: Technology Acquisitions and Military Modernization*. London: Routledge, 2013.

Harris, Shane. *@War: The Rise of the Military-Internet Complex*. New York: Houghton Mifflin Harcourt, 2014.

Hohmann, Mirko, Alexander Pirang and Thorsten Benner. "Advancing Cybersecurity Capacity Building: Implementing a Principle-Based Approach." *Global Public Policy Institute*, March 2017. www.gppi.net/media/Hohmann__Pirang__Benner__2017__Advancing_Cybers ecurity_Capacity_Building.pdf.

Kerala Police. "c0c0n 2020: Keynote Speech by Shri Ajit Doval, National Security Advisor." *YouTube*, September 17, 2020. www.youtube.com/watch?v=m2ctyqdgIzg.

Khanna, Ambika. "India's Evolving Fintech Laws." *Gateway House*, March 14, 2019. www.gatewayhouse.in/indias-fintech-laws/.

Kovacs, Anja. "Is a Reconciliation of Multistakeholderism and Multilateralism in Internet Governance Possible? India at NETmundial." *Internet Democracy Project*. https://internetdemocracy.in/reports/india-at-netmundial/.

Kumar, Aditi and Eric Rosenbach. "The Truth about the Dark Web." *Finance and Development* 56, no. 3 (September 2019): 22–25.

Kushner, David. "The Real Story of Stuxnet." *IEEE Spectrum*, February 26, 2013. https://spectrum.ieee.org/telecom/security/the-real-story-of-stuxnet.

Maimon, David. "Sketchy Darknet Websites Are Taking Advantage of the COVID-19 Pandemic: Buyer Beware." *The Conversation*, August 19, 2020. https://theconversation.com/sketchy-darknet-websites-are-taking-advantage-of-the-covid-19-pandemic-buyer-beware-143237.

Maurer, Tim. *Cyber Mercenaries: The State, Hackers, and Power*. Cambridge: Cambridge University Press, 2018.

Maurer, Tim and Robert Morgus. "Compilation of Existing Cybersecurity and Information Security Related Definitions." *New America*, 2014.

Microsoft. "A Digital Geneva Convention to Protect Cyberspace." Accessed December 29, 2020. https://query.prod.cms.rt.microsoft.com/cms/api/am/binary/RW67QH.

The Ministry of Foreign Affairs and Trade. "Christchurch Call to Eliminate Terrorist and Violent Extremist Content Online." Accessed November 26, 2020. www.christchurchcall.com/call.html.

Nye, Joseph S. "The Regime Complex for Managing Global Cyber Activities." Global Commission on Internet Governance Paper Series No. 1, May 2014. www.cigionline.org/sites/default/files/gcig_paper_no1.pdf.

O'Connor, Sarah, Fergus Hanson, Emilia Currey and Tracy Beattie. "Cyber-Enabled Foreign Interference in Elections and Referendums." *ASPI International Cyber Policy Centre*, Policy Brief Report No. 41/2020. www.aspi.org.au/report/cyber-enabled-foreign-interference-elections-and-referendums.

Omand, David. "The Dark Net: Policing the Internet's Underworld." *World Policy Journal* 32, no. 4 (Winter 2015–16): 75–82.

Patil, Sameer and Sagnik Chakraborty. "A Cybersecurity Agenda for India's Digital Payment Systems." *Gateway House*, Paper no. 20, September 2019. www.gatewayhouse.in/wp-content/uploads/2019/10/Digital-Payments_FINAL.pdf.

Rao, Madanmohan and Osama Manzar, eds. *NetCh@Kra: 15 Years of Internet in India, Retrospect and Roadmaps*. New Delhi: Digital Empowerment Foundation, 2011.

Rao, Prabha. "Online Radicalisation: The Example of Burhan Wani." *Manohar Parrikar Institute for Defence Studies and Analyses*, July 16, 2016. https://idsa.in/issuebrief/online-radicalisation-burhan-wani_prao_160716.

Rosenberg, Matthew, Nicholas Confessore and Carole Cadwalladr. "How Trump Consultants Exploited the Facebook Data of Millions." *The New York Times*, March 17, 2018. www.nytimes.com/2018/03/17/us/politics/cambridge-analytica-trump-campaign.html.

Samuel, Cherian. "Cyber Security: Global, Regional and Local Dynamics." *IDSA* Monograph Series, no. 42 (December 2014).

Saran, Samir. "A Reluctant Digital Power Emerges From the Shadows." *The Wire*, December 22, 2016. https://thewire.in/diplomacy/emergence-reluctant-digital-power.

Schmitt, Michael N. *Tallinn Manual 2.0 on the International Law Applicable to Cyber Operations*. Cambridge, United Kingdom: Cambridge University Press, 2017.

Segal, Adam. *The Hacked World Order*. New York: PublicAffairs, 2016.

United Nations General Assembly. "Group of Governmental Experts on Developments in the Field of Information and Telecommunications in the Context of International Security." Accessed December 29, 2020. www.unidir.org/files/medias/pdfs/developments-in-the-field-of-information-and-telecommunications-in-the-context-of-international-security-2012–2013-a-68–98-eng-0–518.pdf.

UN Secretary-General's High-level Panel on Digital Cooperation. "The Age of Digital Interdependence." Accessed November 26, 2020. www.un.org/en/pdfs/DigitalCooperation-report-for%20web.pdf.

U.S. Senate Select Committee on Intelligence. "Russian Targeting of Election Infrastructure During the 2016 Election: Summary of Initial Findings and Recommendations." Accessed June 15, 2020. www.intelligence.senate.gov/publications/russia-inquiry.

van der Meer, Sico. "How States Could Respond to Non-State Cyber-Attackers." *Clingendael Policy Brief*, June 2020. www.clingendael.org/sites/default/files/2020-06/Policy_Brief_Cyber_non-state_June_2020.pdf.

Weimann, Gabriel. "Terrorist Migration to the Dark Web." *Perspectives on Terrorism* 10, no. 3 (2016): 40–44.

Index

Note: Page numbers in *italics* indicates figures and page numbers in **bold** indicates tables.

Aadhaar-enabled Payment Systems (AEPS) 34
Advanced Persistent Threat (APT) 1, **38**, **39**, **40**, **41**; APT30 14, 15; APT38 35
advance-fee scams 13, 20n3
Ansar Ghazwatul Hind 54
Anthem **4**, 36
APM Terminals 15
Aramco **3**, 7
attribution 6, 7; India and 16, 60; problem of 2

Bangladesh Bank 2, **4**
BHIM Aadhaar Pay 34, **38**
Bitcoin **4**, 35, **49**, 50; *see also* crypto-currencies
Budapest Convention on Cybercrime, of Council of Europe 9, 61

Cambridge Analytica 26
Carbanak **3**, 35
Central Monitoring System (CMS) 19
Centre for Development of Advanced Computing (C-DAC) *17*, 18, 28, 64
China 1, 7, 8, 9, 10; and attack on Office of Personnel Management **4**; and cyber attacks on India 16; and G20 Digital Economy Task Force 64; involvement in espionage 6
Christchurch Call to Action 60
City Union Bank **15**, 36
Committee on Internet-related Policies (CIRP), of UN 61–62
Cooperative Cyber Defence Centre of Excellence, of North Atlantic Treaty Organization 8
Cosmos Bank 15, 36

Covid-19 1, 26, 52
Crimea *see* Ukraine
critical infrastructure 22–23; GGE and 8
critical sectors 23
crypto-currencies **49**, 50; India and 35, **43**
Cyber Diplomacy division, of MEA 18
Cyberdome 18
cyber-enabled espionage 6, 8, 14, **15**, **38**
cyber-enabled propaganda *see* disinformation
cyber hygiene 19, 30, 37, **38**, **39**, **40**

Daesh 7, 16, 53, 54
dark net 16, 48, 50, 53–54, 55
dark net marketplaces *see* digital black markets
data localisation 42, **44**, 61
deep web 47, 48, 54
Defence Cyber Agency *17*, 18
Democratic National Committee **4**, 26
digital black markets 16, **41**, 50–54
Digital Geneva Convention 9
digital payment systems 34
disinformation 6, 26, 27
Distributed Denial of Service (DDoS) **3**, **4**, 14, 26, **41**
doxing 7, **38**, **39**, **40**
Duqu **3**, 24

e-commerce 50, 61, 64
Education and Research Network (Ernet) 13
Election Commission of India 27
election infrastructure 7, 26–27
encryption 48
Estonia **3**, 8–9
Europol 55
exit scam 48, 50, 55

Facebook 6, 26–27, 48, 54
fake news 26, 27
Federal Bureau of Investigation (FBI) 50, 55
Federal Reserve Bank **4**; *see also* Bangladesh Bank
FireEye 1, 2, **5**, 9, 14

Gill, Amandeep Singh 61
Global Commission on Internet Governance 9
Global Commission on the Stability of Cyberspace 9
Global Forum on Cyber Expertise (GFCE) 63
Group of Governmental Experts (GGE), of United Nations (UN) 7–8, 60, 61
Google 6, 47

High-Level Panel on Digital Cooperation, of UN 9, 61
Hitachi Payment Systems 14, **15**, 36
Huawei 6
hybrid warfare 7, 26

Indian Banks-Center for Analysis of Risks and Threats (IB-CART) 42
Indian Computer Emergency Response Team (CERT-IN) 16, *17*, 18, 19; and attacks on SCADA systems 26; and digital payment systems 42, **43**; and participation in multilateral technical forums 64; and Stuxnet infections 24
Indian Cyber Crime Coordination Centre (I4C) *17*, 18, 54
Indian Technical and Economic Cooperation *see* Ministry of External Affairs (MEA)
IndiaStack 33, 64
Industrial Control Systems **3**, 14
Information Technology (IT) Act 2000 16, 19, 22, 42
insider threat 24, 40
Institute for Development & Research in Banking Technology (IDRBT) 42
Intelligence Bureau *17*, 18, 19
Intermediary Guidelines 19
International Telecommunications Union (ITU) 60, 64
Internet Corporation for Assigned Names and Numbers (ICANN) 62
Iran **3**, **5**, 7, 24, 48
Islamic State *see* Daesh
Israel 2, 7, 24

Jaish-e-Mohammed 16
JAM trinity 34
Japan *see* Mt. Gox
Jawaharlal Nehru Port Trust *see* APM Terminals

Kim, Jong–Un 3
Kudankulam nuclear reactor **15**, 26

Lashkar-e-Taiba 16
Lazarus group 2, **4**, 36
lemonising tactic 55

Maersk 2
Maharashtra Cyber 18
malware 2, 14, 26, 36, 37
Mandiant 6; *see also* FireEye
Man in the middle attack **38**, **39**, **41**
Microsoft **5**, 6, 9
Ministry of Defence (MoD) 16, *17*, 18
Ministry of Electronics and Information Technology (MEITY) 13, 16, *17*, 18, 59
Ministry of External Affairs (MEA) *17*, 18, 59, 62, 64
Ministry of Finance (MoF) 16, *17*, 18
Ministry of Home Affairs (MHA) 16, *17*, 18, 54, 55
mobile wallets *see* Prepaid Payment Instruments (PPI)
Mt. Gox **4**

Narcotics Control Bureau (NCB) 53, 54, 55
National Crime Records Bureau *17*, 18
National Critical Information Infrastructure Protection Centre (NCIIPC) *17*, 18, 27, 28, **43**
National Cybercrime Reporting portal 18, 54
National Cyber Security Coordinator (NCSC) 16, *17*, 19
National Cyber Security Policy (NCSP) 16, 42
National Informatics Centre *17*, 18
National Payments Corporation of India (NPCI) 34
National Research Council, of Canada 7
National Security Advisor 16, *17*, 26
National Security Agency (NSA), of the US 5, 6, 9
National Security Council Secretariat (NSCS) 16, *17*, 27
National Technical Research Organisation (NTRO) *17*, 18, 27

Nigerian phishing scam 14
North Korea 2, **3**, **4**, 6, 26, 35
NotPetya 2, **5**

Open-Ended Working Group, of UN 8, 61
Osaka Track for Data Governance 61

Pakistan 13, 16
Paris Call 9
Petya **5**, **15**
phishing **15**, 36, 37
Point of Sale (PoS) terminal 34
Prepaid Payment Instruments (PPI) 35, **39**, 42
Pretty Good Privacy (PGP) **49**
PRISM surveillance programme, of NSA 6

Quadrilateral Security Initiative 63

ransomware **5**, **15**, **16**, 36
Research and Analysis Wing *17*, 18
Reserve Bank of India (RBI) *17*, 18, 34, 35, 42, **43**, **44**
Reserve Bank Information Technology Private Limited (ReBIT) *17*, 18, 42
RuPay 34
Russia 2, **3**, **4**, **5**, 7, 10; and APTs 1; and cyber attack on Ukraine 25–26; and cyber attacks on US 6; and interference in US presidential elections 26–27; and management of cyber space 8, 61, 62; and TOR traffic 48

Saudi Arabia *see* Aramco
sectoral CERT 28, 45
Siemens 6, 24
Silk Road marketplaces 50, **51**, 55
Snowden, Edward 6
social engineering 13, 36, 50

Sony 2, **3**, **4**
Supervisory Control and Data Acquisition (SCADA) 14, 23–28
Stuxnet 2, 6, 7, 8, 14, 23–24
SWIFT **4**, 35, 42, **44**
Symantec 24

Tallinn Manual 9, 61
Tech Accords 9
The Onion Router (TOR) 16, 47–54
Twitter 48, 54

Ukraine **4**, **5**, 25–26
Ulbricht, Ross **51**
Unified Payments Interface (UPI) 34, **38**
Union Bank of India **15**, 36
Unique Identification Authority of India (UIDAI) *17*, 18
United Nations Office on Drugs and Crime 55
United States (US) **3**, **4**, **5**, 7; and attribution 2; and China's cyber espionage 6; and crackdown on dark net marketplaces 50; and cyber attack on government agencies 2; and cyber security cooperation with India 63; and management of cyber space 7, 8, 61; and Russian interference in presidential elections 26, 27; and Stuxnet 24; and TOR 48, 49
Unstructured Supplementary Service Data (USSD) **34**, **38**
US Naval Research Laboratory 47

Virtual Private Network (VPN) 48, 54, 56

WannaCry 2, **5**, 6, 9, **15**, 20
World Summit on the Information Society (WSIS) 60, 61
World Trade Organization (WTO) 61, 64